**New Directions for
Student Services**

John H. Schuh
EDITOR-IN-CHIEF

Elizabeth J. Whitt
ASSOCIATE EDITOR

Supporting Graduate and Professional Students: The Role of Student Affairs

Melanie J. Guentzel
Becki Elkins Nesheim
EDITORS

Number 115 • Fall 2006
Jossey-Bass
San Francisco

SUPPORTING GRADUATE AND PROFESSIONAL STUDENTS: THE ROLE OF
STUDENT AFFAIRS
Melanie J. Guentzel, Becki Elkins Nesheim (eds.)
New Directions for Student Services, no. 115
John H. Schuh, Editor-in-Chief
Elizabeth J. Whitt, Associate Editor

NEW DIRECTIONS FOR STUDENT SERVICES (ISSN 0164-7970, e-ISSN 1536-
0695) is part of The Jossey-Bass Higher and Adult Education Series and
is published quarterly by Wiley Subscription Services, Inc., A Wiley Company, at Jossey-Bass, 989 Market Street, San Francisco, California 94103-
1741. Periodicals Postage Paid at San Francisco, California, and at
additional mailing offices. POSTMASTER: Send address changes to New
Directions for Student Services, Jossey-Bass, 989 Market Street, San Francisco, CA 94103-1741.

New Directions for Student Services is indexed in College Student Personnel Abstracts and Contents Pages in Education.

Microfilm copies of issues and articles are available in 16mm and 35mm,
as well as microfiche in 105mm, through University Microfims Inc., 300
North Zeeb Road, Ann Arbor, Michigan 48106-1346.

SUBSCRIPTIONS cost $80 for individuals and $190 for institutions, agencies,
and libraries. See ordering information page at end of book.

EDITORIAL CORRESPONDENCE should be sent to the Editor-in-Chief, John
H. Schuh, N 243 Lagomarcino Hall, Iowa State University, Ames, Iowa
50011.

www.josseybass.com

CONTENTS

EDITORS' NOTES

The historical focus of student affairs has been on understanding and meeting the needs of traditional-aged undergraduate students. Although shifts in the demographic characteristics of enrolled students have broadened the definition of college students, student affairs practice has continued to emphasize undergraduate education. Student affairs professionals traditionally have viewed graduate and professional students and their needs as the responsibility of individual academic departments or the graduate college.

Only recently has the graduate student come to the attention of the student affairs profession. The desire on the part of student affairs professionals for information about working with graduate and professional students is evident in the increased number of presentations on the topic at national conferences over the past five years. In addition, both the National Association for Student Personnel Administrators (NASPA) and the American College Personnel Association (ACPA) have established new networks designed to serve the needs and interests of student affairs professionals who work with graduate and professional students. NASPA's Administrators in Graduate and Professional Student Services (AGAPSS) Knowledge Community and ACPA's Commission for Graduate and Professional School Educators call attention to the growing recognition of the needs of graduate and professional students.

Much of the available research on graduate education highlights the departmental role in supporting the academic experience. This volume instead focuses on the needs of graduate and professional students that can be addressed specifically by student affairs professionals. The education of graduate and professional students is labor intensive on the part of faculty, with an assumption made that academic departments support students academically, socially, and professionally. However, education within the academy can be a fragmented learning experience (Chickering and Gamson, 1991).

This fragmentation might be even more descriptive of the graduate experience where academic departments emphasize the cognitive intellectual development of a scholar rather than the psychosocial aspects of the graduate student experience. We know from research on undergraduate students and on nontraditional-aged learners that learning occurs holistically and within the context of a student's life experience (Pascarella and Terenzini, 1991, 2005). We also know that student development continues beyond the undergraduate experience and that graduate students continue to make

WILEY InterScience®
DISCOVER SOMETHING GREAT

New Directions for Student Services, no. 115, Fall 2006   © Wiley Periodicals, Inc.
Published online in Wiley InterScience (www.interscience.wiley.com) • DOI: 10.1002/ss.211

meaning of experiences with diversity and processes of self-authorship (Baxter Magolda, 1998; McEwen and Roper, 1994). The research on doctoral students in particular indicates a need for support beyond the academic experience with a role for student affairs professionals to play in the development of the whole graduate student (Golde and Dore, 2001; Fischer and Zigmond, 1998).

In our initial proposal for this volume, we suggested focusing on doctoral students, as much of the research on graduate students does. When asked to expand our focus to include the broader graduate and professional student population, we agreed. To the extent that it simplifies the issues and homogenizes the population, the broad term *graduate students* makes our task easier. Much of the research available refers to graduate students as a monolithic whole, encompassing master's students, doctoral students, and professional students. While simpler, this is much like studying elephants, polar bears, and lemurs as members of the animal kingdom to identify their common needs.

Graduate students in general are a heterogeneous group, more different than alike across programmatic types, disciplinary affiliations, and individual characteristics and experiences. One size does not fit all when it comes to services, but there are some strategic areas where departments and student affairs can have an effect (Fischer and Zigmond, 1998). Identified areas of need that hold specific interest for student affairs include orientation, advising and registration, financial aid and financial planning, community building, social interaction and activities, counseling, and professional development and career planning (Austin, 2002; Baird, 1993; Boyle and Boice, 1998; Lipschutz, 1993; Nerad and Cerny, 1993; Nyquist and others, 1999).

Because one size will not fit all master's, doctoral, and professional students, we advise professionals working with graduate students or institutions interested in better serving their graduate populations to learn who their students are and ask them about their specific needs. To this end, we begin this volume with a chapter on identifying the needs of graduate and professional students. Becki Elkins Nesheim, Melanie Guentzel, Ann Gansemer-Topf, Leah Ewing Ross, and Cathryn Turrentine discuss in Chapter One the role of assessment and provide examples of one research study and an assessment project designed to identify the needs and experiences of graduate and professional students. Suggestions for planning, implementing, and reporting the results of assessment efforts to improve graduate education are outlined.

The next three chapters provide some context for graduate education. In Chapter Two, Ann Gansemer-Topf, Leah Ewing Ross, and R. M. Johnson offer a brief review of the literature related to the psychological, social, and cognitive aspects of graduate and professional student development. This chapter provides a developmental framework with which to examine the proposed areas of intervention. Chris Peterson Brus, in Chapter Three, examines the changing graduate student population and explores the educational equity challenges created for nontraditional graduate students as they strive to balance academic rigor and lives outside the academy. In

Chapter Four, Jason Pontius and Shaun Harper identify principles for good practice for graduate student engagement.

The balance of the chapters explores programming and services designed to meet the needs of graduate and professional students. In Chapter Five, Linda McGuire and Julie Phye discuss the concept of professionalism as a common concern for the medical and legal professions and examine approaches taken within a college of medicine and a college of law to infuse professionalism into the student experience. Tom Lekher and Jennifer Furlong, in Chapter Six, highlight and offer strategies to meet the career development needs of graduate students. In Chapter Seven, Lisa Brandes looks at the movement to create graduate student centers and how these centers of people, space, and programming meet student needs.

In the final chapter, we synthesize the conclusions drawn across the chapters, identifying common themes. We conclude with recommendations for practice in graduate student services based on the identified themes.

Melanie J. Guentzel
Becki Elkins Nesheim
Editors

References

Austin, A. E. "Preparing the Next Generation of Faculty: Graduate School as Socialization to the Academic Career." *Journal of Higher Education,* 2002, 73(1), 94–122.

Baird, L. L. "Using Research and Theoretical Models of Graduate Student Progress." In L. J. Baird (ed.), *Increasing Graduate Student Retention and Degree Attainment.* New Directions for Institutional Research, no. 80. San Francisco: Jossey-Bass, 1993.

Baxter Magolda, M. B. "Developing Self-Authorship in Graduate School." In M. S. Anderson (ed.), *The Experience of Being in Graduate School: An Exploration.* New Directions for Higher Education, no. 101. San Francisco: Jossey-Bass, 1998.

Boyle, P., and Boice, B. "Best Practices for Enculturation: Collegiality, Mentoring, and Structure." In M. S. Anderson (ed.), *The Experience of Being in Graduate School: An Exploration.* New Directions for Higher Education, no. 101. San Francisco: Jossey-Bass, 1998.

Chickering, A. W., and Gamson, Z. F. (eds.). *New Directions for Teaching and Learning— Applying the Seven Principles for Good Practice in Undergraduate Education.* San Francisco: Jossey-Bass, 1991.

Fischer, B. A., and Zigmond, M. J. "Survival Skills for Graduate School and Beyond." In M. S. Anderson (ed.), *The Experience of Being in Graduate School: An Exploration.* New Directions for Higher Education, no. 101. San Francisco: Jossey-Bass, 1998.

Golde, C. M., and Dore, T. M. "At Cross Purposes: What the Experiences of Today's Doctoral Students Reveal About Doctoral Education." 2001. Retrieved Aug. 30, 2005, from http://www.phd-survey.org.

Lipschutz, S. S. "Enhancing Success in Doctoral Education: From Policy to Practice." In L. J. Baird (ed.), *Increasing Graduate Student Retention and Degree Attainment.* New Directions for Institutional Research, no. 80. San Francisco: Jossey-Bass, 1993.

McEwen, M. J., and Roper, L. "Interracial Experiences, Knowledge, and Skills of Master's Degree Students in Graduate Programs in Student Affairs." *Journal of College Student Development,* 1994, 35(2), 81–87.

Nerad, M., and Cerny, J. "From Facts to Action: Expanding the Graduate Division's Educational Role." In L. J. Baird (ed.), *Increasing Graduate Student Retention and Degree*

Attainment. New Directions for Institutional Research, no. 80. San Francisco: Jossey-Bass, 1993.

Nyquist, J. D., and others. "On the Road to Becoming a Professor." *Change,* 1999, *31*(3), 18–27.

Pascarella, E. T., and Terenzini, P. T. *How College Affects Students.* San Francisco: Jossey-Bass, 1991.

Pascarella, E. T., and Terenzini, P. T. *How College Affects Students: A Third Decade of Research.* San Francisco: Jossey-Bass, 2005.

MELANIE J. GUENTZEL is director of graduate student services at St. Cloud State University and a doctoral candidate in student affairs administration and research at the University of Iowa.

BECKI ELKINS NESHEIM is the director of institutional research at Cornell College in Mount Vernon, Iowa.

NEW DIRECTIONS FOR STUDENT SERVICES • DOI: 10.1002/ss

1

In order to design effective interventions for working with graduate and professional students, educators must first assess students' needs and experiences. This chapter highlights the importance of assessment in graduate and professional education and offers insights gained from three studies.

If You Want to Know, Ask: Assessing the Needs and Experiences of Graduate Students

Becki Elkins Nesheim, Melanie J. Guentzel, Ann M. Gansemer-Topf, Leah Ewing Ross, Cathryn G. Turrentine

Assessment has become an essential part of undergraduate education. To address issues of accountability, educators increasingly rely on assessment efforts to demonstrate student learning outcomes both in and out of class. Perhaps as a result of not being highlighted in the calls for educational reform, graduate education has not been quick to embrace assessment of programs, practices, or outcomes (Haworth, 1996). This chapter seeks to encourage educators working with graduate and professional students to engage in assessment to find out who students are, what they identify as needs at their institution, and what they are learning. We begin with a discussion of research on graduate students and move to an exploration of assessing the needs and experiences of graduate and professional students. The chapter outlines three sample studies and offers strategies for conducting successful assessment projects with graduate students.

Research on Graduate Students

Research on graduate students is clustered in four areas: student attrition and persistence (Baird, 1993; Golde, 1998; Lovitts, 2001, Tinto, 1993), learning experiences (Anderson and Swazey, 1998; Baxter Magolda, 1998;

NEW DIRECTIONS FOR STUDENT SERVICES, no. 115, Fall 2006 © Wiley Periodicals, Inc.
Published online in Wiley InterScience (www.interscience.wiley.com) • DOI: 10.1002/ss.212

Golde and Dore, 2001; Owen, 1999), socialization (Austin, 2002; Boyle and Boice, 1998; Nyquist and others, 1999; Weidman, Twale, and Stein, 2001), and programmatic interventions (Forney and Davis, 2002; Herman and Hazler, 1999; Lee and Graham, 2001; Poock, 2002, 2004). We briefly examine each of these areas to help frame the assessments of the graduate and professional student experiences described in this chapter.

Although we refer to the graduate and professional student experience, this experience is not monolithic. Graduate and professional students are an extremely heterogeneous group of people pursuing degrees beyond the baccalaureate in diverse institutional, geographical, disciplinary, and cultural settings. For this reason, assessment must be undertaken at each individual institution. General research on graduate and professional students can guide assessment and inform interventions but should not be assumed to accurately reflect students on individual campuses. The purpose of this review is to examine the existing research on graduate students, briefly look at the types of assessments of the graduate student experience conducted at graduate institutions, and illustrate why individual institutional assessment is essential.

Student Attrition. One of the most studied areas of graduate education is that of attrition and persistence. Concern about attrition stems from a recognition of the cost to the institution and the student in terms of time and money. The further students get into the doctorate or professional degree, the greater the time and expense put into the degree by the student and the institution. Bowen and Rudenstine (1992) noted that "ideally, those who eventually drop out should do so as early as possible in order to minimize this loss" (p. 112). Resource investments, on the part of both students and institutions, motivate the study of student attrition.

It is difficult to determine the doctoral attrition rate because time to degree completion ranges, on average, from eight years (in science) to twelve years (in the humanities) past the baccalaureate degree. Nonetheless, attrition rates for doctoral students in all fields hover at about 50 percent (Bowen and Rudenstine, 1992; Lovitts, 2001; Tinto, 1993). In terms of the breakdown of attrition, one-third of doctoral students who leave do so after year one, one-third leave prior to course completion, and the final third leave prior to completion of the dissertation (Bowen and Rudenstine, 1992).

Attrition is often identified as an individual issue, removing responsibility for the loss from the department (Golde, 1996, 1998; Lovitts, 1996, 2001; Nerad and Miller, 1996). Departments try to address attrition by changing admission standards to enroll "better" students (Lovitts, 2001). This strategy rationalizes that admitting better and better-prepared students will minimize the number of students who leave.

Responsibility for student success, however, does not lie solely with the student (Golde, 1998). Lovitts and Nelson (2000), in their review of the results of two studies of graduate students, asserted that attrition is not the result of admitting poor students but the result of poor programmatic experiences. They noted, "Students leave less because of what they bring with them to the university than because of what happens to them after they arrive" (p. 50). In fact, they found that students who leave have higher grade point averages and are more often women or students of color. They attribute student attrition to a lack of integration into the graduate program resulting from the organizational and social structures of graduate education and the culture of graduate school.

Student Experiences. The research on student experiences often occurs as an extension of the focus on attrition. This research seeks to find out what students are experiencing in their graduate programs for purposes of understanding what makes them leave or stay. Golde and Dore (2001), for instance, conducted a national study of doctoral education and career preparation that illuminated some concerns for graduate education. Doctoral students in eleven disciplines in the arts and sciences at twenty-seven institutions were surveyed about their reasons for pursuing a doctorate, the effectiveness of their programs, and their expectations and understanding of programs. The study found several mismatches between student expectations and reality, noting that students were missing information about the "time, money, clarity of purpose and perseverance doctoral education entails" (p. 33). Students did not have realistic expectations of the scope of doctoral study, the careers they sought were not widely available, and they were not being prepared for the jobs they took.

This research also explores students' experiences in graduate education in general. These studies answer the question, "What's happening here?" An earlier study of the doctoral experience surveyed two thousand students from ninety-nine departments in chemistry, civil engineering, microbiology, and sociology (Anderson and Swazey, 1998). Anderson and Swazey asked students why they went to graduate school, what they thought of their academic work, their perceptions of the departmental climate, the personal effects of graduate work, and their beliefs about degree completion. This quantitative study offered a snapshot of the student experience across departments at several major research universities. A national qualitative case study of master's programs conducted by Conrad, Haworth, and Millar (1993) examined how those involved in master's education interpreted and evaluated the master's experience and what characteristics they believed enhanced the quality of the experience. They found that "master's education in the United States has been a silent success for degree holders, employers and society in general" (p. 315). These studies, and others like them, illuminate graduate education as experienced by students.

Socialization to a Profession. Socialization theory provides a useful framework for examining the graduate student experience (Baird, 1990; Golde, 1998). Graduate and professional education are designed to socialize students to the values and culture of a profession (Boyle and Boice, 1998; Golde, 1998; Weidman, Twale, and Stein, 2001). Socialization constitutes a process that includes ongoing transitions as students progress and face new challenges. Van Maanen and Schein (1979) discussed the socialization

NEW DIRECTIONS FOR STUDENT SERVICES • DOI: 10.1002/ss

process as one of divestiture, where one removes the previous self-concept and takes on a new view of the self that reflects the new group membership (Anderson and Swazey, 1998).

Particularly in the first year, new skills must be learned and adjustments to new environments must be made. Indeed, Tinto (1994) identified the first year as a "transition to membership in the graduate community" (Baird, 1993, p. 7). Students are in the process of developing relationships with faculty and fellow students and determining how the norms and values of the department meld with their own values. This process of values identification and adjustment can be painful. Nyquist and others (1999) found that for some students, coming to terms with the values of the academy involved disillusionment and a setting aside of their own values, while for others values meshed well and the academy's values were easily internalized.

Weidman, Twale, and Stein (2001) offered a dynamic and nonlinear model that illustrates the complexity involved in socialization to a profession. They asserted that socialization is an interactive process between the person and the socializing factors of time, location, and experiences. (This model is discussed more fully in this volume in Chapter Two.) As we assess student learning and student experiences, it is useful to incorporate this complexity into the interpretation of gathered information.

Programming for Graduate Students. The final cluster of research entails studies conducted to assess the impact of programmatic interventions. Much of this research looks at co-curricular services such as orientation (Barker, Felstehausen, Couch, and Henry, 1997; Forney and Davis, 2002; Owen, 1999; Poock, 2002) and wellness and counseling services (Group for the Advancement of Psychiatry, 1999; Herman and Hazler, 1999; Hodgson and Simoni, 1995; Lee and Graham, 2001) at individual institutions. These studies illustrate strategies for assessing the outcomes of specific interventions on the graduate and professional student experience.

Research Summary. The research on graduate students focuses on attrition, student experiences, socialization, and programmatic interventions. Although useful, this research tells educators very little about the needs and experiences of students at their particular institutions. Tailoring programs and services for graduate and professional students necessitates first taking steps to assess the needs and experiences of such students on individual campuses. If we are interested in designing services to retain graduate and professional students, we must begin by asking them about their needs and experiences (Haworth, 1996; Nerad and Miller, 1996). The remainder of this chapter explores the role of assessment in graduate education.

Assessing Student Needs and Experiences

Assessment has come to play an increasingly important role in student affairs practice. Upcraft and Schuh (1996) defined assessment as "any effort to gather, analyze, and interpret evidence which describes institutional, divisional, or agency effectiveness" (p. 18). General assessment efforts exist in higher education for purposes of enhancing student learning and development (Palomba, 2001).

More specifically, needs assessment serves a critical role in higher education (Banta, 2002; Schuh and Upcraft, 2001; Soriano, 1995; Upcraft and Schuh, 1996). Banta (2002), calling on the work of Brent Ruben, maintained that educators "should study the needs and perceptions of those we intend to serve and identify gaps between what we think we are doing and how we are perceived by our constituents, and take action designed to reduce the gaps" (p. 285). A systematic needs assessment naturally should precede the development of any new program or service (Schuh and Upcraft, 2001). Assessment of students' needs is closely related to the assessment of students' satisfaction with their educational experiences, satisfaction resulting to a large degree from an institutional or organizational ability to meet their needs (Schuh and Upcraft, 2001).

Whereas the discussion of assessment in higher education has emphasized undergraduate education, little information is available about assessment activities focused at the graduate level. Assessment of needs and experiences, however, is essential to providing quality services to graduate students. The following section outlines three studies designed to understand graduate students' needs and experiences.

Assessment Examples. Studies were completed at three institutions, one at a Master's College/University-I in the Northeast and two at Doctoral Extensive institutions in the Midwest. (The names of the institutions have been changed for this chapter.) Two of the studies began as research endeavors. They are included here because of the lessons learned that pertain to assessment.

Yankee State University. A year-long assessment and policy development project was conducted at a master's-level institution in the Northeast. The Graduate Student Services Project was designed to enhance administrative and support services for graduate students. The project included assessment of graduate student needs and the development of recommendations to address those needs. To complete the study, four processes occurred: (1) individual interviews with sixty-one graduate program coordinators, faculty, administrators, and support staff members; (2) benchmarking with nine peer institutions; (3) focus group interviews with graduate students; and (4) development of recommendations by a twelve-member working group. Only the graduate student focus groups and the recommendation working group are described in greater detail here.

Ten focus groups were conducted with 119 graduate students, including students pursuing master's degrees and Certificates of Advanced Graduate Study (CAGS). Focus groups occurred with academic courses, one student organization, and three other specific groups of graduate students. Purposive sampling was used to identify participant groups that would best represent the YSU graduate student population. Participant groups included on-campus and off-campus classes; classes in each academic college; first-year, second-year, and CAGS-level classes; and classes with large numbers of nonmatriculated students. Full-time and part-time students, international students, graduate assistants, and graduate students of color participated. Students were asked to identify which administrative and support services were most helpful to them, as well as those that were least helpful or not working well. Students were asked to review a list of issues identified in the administrative interviews for relevance to their experiences. Focus group interviews were audiorecorded, transcribed, and analyzed for emerging themes.

To complete the study, a working group of twelve members was convened to discuss the results and formulate recommendations for the institution. The group consisted of the researcher, graduate program coordinators from each academic college, an associate academic dean, a faculty member, four administrators, two support staff members, and a graduate student. The group emphasized reaching consensus on each recommendation. Each recommendation was subject to rigorous discussion and negotiation, with each group member having the authority to veto any recommendation.

University of the Midwest. The assessment project at University of the Midwest (UM) originated as a research study. The purpose of the study, as presented for human subjects approval, was to understand the needs and experiences of the institution's doctoral students. The study sought to understand (1) how doctoral students described their experiences as graduate students, (2) the factors they identified as facilitating their progress toward degree completion, (3) the factors they identified as inhibiting progress, and (4) their articulated needs.

Initial student recruitment efforts began by targeting specific departments: math, chemistry, English, communication studies, curriculum and instruction, and psychological and quantitative foundations. Departments varied in their willingness to provide the names and e-mail addresses of their doctoral students or to allow the posting of fliers announcing the focus group dates and times. An initial round of focus group interviews was conducted with only one student participating. Subsequent recruitment efforts incorporated assistance from the registrar's office and entailed sending a mass e-mail to all registered doctoral students at UM. The e-mail message announced the study, invited participants, and requested students to respond to a specific focus group date and time. A second round of six focus groups was conducted during the summer, with approximately thirty students participating.

Student participants were enrolled in the following degree programs: biomedical engineering, neuroscience, business, accounting, speech pathology, math education, rehabilitation counseling, student affairs administration and research, foreign language acquisition research and education, psychology, and engineering. Participants were asked to describe their experiences as graduate students, identify factors that supported or inhibited

NEW DIRECTIONS FOR STUDENT SERVICES • DOI: 10.1002/ss

their progress, and specify the needs they believed a hypothetical graduate student services office should address. Interviews were audiorecorded and transcribed. Data were analyzed for emerging themes.

Midwestern State University. As with the study at UM, the project at Midwestern State University (MSU) also began as a research study to understand the experiences and needs of doctoral students. This study was conducted in collaboration with the UM study and therefore sought to achieve the same purposes as those identified above.

Researchers began identifying participants through a course on preparing future faculty and personal contacts with faculty members and graduate students. Through these interactions, the researchers received a list of the directors of graduate education (DOGEs). Because DOGEs would not provide lists of their graduate students but would forward a recruitment message to them, the researchers sent one e-mail message to all DOGEs with a request to forward the message to graduate students. The forwarded message requested student participation in the study.

Through this process, six focus group interviews were coordinated and conducted over the course of one week, with approximately thirty students participating. Degree programs represented were biochemistry, physics, mechanical engineering, agronomy, immunobiology, economics, genetics, bioinformatics and computational biology, sociology, human development and family studies, educational leadership, and political science. Interviews were audiorecorded and transcribed, with data analyzed for emerging themes. In addition, a faculty member in the College of Education allowed one of the researchers to conduct a focus group with class participants. Interviews were audiorecorded and transcribed, with data analyzed for emerging themes.

Assessment Strategies. In *Assessment Practice in Student Affairs,* Schuh and Upcraft (2001) outlined practical steps to follow in designing assessment studies: (1) define the problem, (2) identify the study's purpose, (3) determine where to get necessary information, (4) determine the best assessment methods, (5) determine whom to study, (6) specify how data will be collected, (7) identify the instruments or protocols to be used, (8) determine who should collect the data, (9) identify how the data will be analyzed, (10) specify the study's implications for policy and practice, and (11) effectively report the results. These steps provide a framework to guide assessment projects focused on graduate students. Lessons learned from the three studies suggest additional points for consideration in assessing the needs and experiences of graduate students.

Consider Access and Timing. Gaining access to graduate students can be challenging for a number of reasons. First, tracking graduate students through academic records presents a host of problems, given that time to degree completion varies widely (Bowen and Rudenstine, 1992) and that students occasionally change their degree aspirations without updating their records. Second, access can depend largely on the extent to which the study has been sanctioned by the institution or key constituents. Consider, for example, the differences in access to students between the Yankee State University study and the two doctoral student studies. The YSU assessment investigator had access to graduate students through courses and student organizations because of institutional support. In contrast, the MSU and UM investigators had to rely on mass e-mail announcements, personal connections, and word-of-mouth advertising to recruit student participants.

Third, who is conducting the study can play a role in gaining access to students. Several students in the UM study, for instance, chose to participate to support the research efforts of the investigators, with whom they identified as doctoral students. At the same time, however, the fact that the investigators were doctoral students raised issues of credibility and hindered their ability to gain access to students through academic departments.

Finally, timing of the study can inhibit or enhance student participation. Without access to students through courses, timing of focus groups or survey administration is critical. Our experiences suggest that graduate students are less likely to respond at the beginning or end of academic terms. Because many graduate students are involved in teaching and research, the beginning and end of semesters can be busy as they prepare for or complete their assistantship work. The time of day during which focus groups are held also warrants consideration. For instance, many institutions or departments enroll part-time students who are employed full time and attend classes in the evenings or on weekends. These students are unlikely to attend daytime interviews.

To address access concerns, assessors should consider the following issues. First, who are the researchers involved in the study? How are the individuals involved likely to inhibit or enhance access to, and involvement of, students? What credibility concerns or issues of trust are likely to arise based on the investigators' characteristics?

Second, what current and operationalized structures or activities can provide access to graduate students? For instance, does the institution have annual training sessions for graduate assistants, or do academic departments require student enrollment in orientation seminars for first-year graduate students? Does the institution have the capacity for mass e-mailing select students? Tapping into these resources may save time and energy in collecting data, as well as provide a more comprehensive sample of graduate students.

Third, what graduate student networks exist, and how might they be used to foster student participation? Finally, when are graduate students available and most likely to participate in a study?

Involve Stakeholders. Effective assessment projects involve important constituents from the beginning (Banta, 2002; Palomba, 2001; Schuh and Upcraft, 2000, 2001). Involving stakeholders early in the conception of the study serves to build necessary support and address potential points of opposition (Schuh and Upcraft, 2000). In assessment discussions, however, stakeholders are often identified as senior leadership, administrators, staff, faculty, and, in some cases, external audiences.

Assessment projects designed to attend to graduate students must involve graduate students as stakeholders. In addition to the general insights they can provide about graduate education, graduate student members of the assessment team can provide credibility with other students and likely can help maneuver existing graduate student networks. Furthermore, graduate student stakeholders can provide an important voice in the interpretive and recommendation phases of the project, as in the case of the Yankee State study. One note of caution is warranted, however. Often as student affairs professionals, we tend to seek involvement from graduate students in our college student personnel or higher education programs. It is important, in this case, to involve graduate students from other academic disciplines as a means to provide a broader understanding of the graduate student experience.

Pay Attention to the Political Landscape of Graduate Education. All assessment takes place in a political context that must be considered during design, implementation, and reporting of the results (Schuh and Upcraft, 2000, 2001). Graduate education offers its own unique political landscape to which student affairs professionals assessing student needs and experiences must attend. Unlike undergraduate education, which tends to be viewed as an institutionwide endeavor, graduate education falls largely to the purview of academic departments (Pruitt-Logan and Isaac, 1995). Understanding the role and the political dynamics of the graduate college, academic departments, and the faculty is critical to the success of any assessment project. These factors can contribute to or deter from one's ability to gain access to graduate students or to involve stakeholders.

Graduate student participants repeatedly reminded us of the risks they assumed by taking part in these studies. Several students in the UM study, for instance, noted that their faculty advisors would be disturbed to know they were participating in focus groups and would want to be informed about the exact nature of the discussion. Students sharing their experiences risk being viewed as complainers or as disloyal to an advisor or a department. For many students, advisors hold a great deal of power and are capable of making or breaking not only a graduate career but future careers as well.

Individuals interested in assessing graduate education must understand such power dynamics and potential conflicts of interest at play for participants and take necessary steps to prevent or minimize risks (Schuh and Upcraft, 2000). Although qualitative research methods mandate measures to protect participant confidentiality (Marshall and Rossman, 1999; Merriam, 1998), additional steps might be necessary to minimize actual or perceived risks. It might prove important, for instance, to consider the location of the interviews for political implications. Students might feel more comfortable, and be more likely to participate, if interviews are held in a commons space, such as a college union, as opposed to conference rooms located in or near their academic departments. In this case, a location that at first glance appears more convenient for students might ultimately deter student participation. Throughout the assessment process, consideration must be given to the political nature of assessment, particularly as it affects graduate students.

Know What You Are Doing with the Information. Graduate students who participated in these studies, particularly those who attended focus groups outside of courses or organizations, expressed a desire to know the outcomes of the studies. Many expected the results would be used to improve the educational experiences of graduate students, even if that had not been part of the study purpose. A few students, although willing participants, shared an attitude of "nothing matters," meaning that nothing could or would be done to improve their experiences. These students assumed that individuals in a position to effect change were not interested in hearing from graduate students.

Our experiences suggested, however, that most graduate students took their roles in these studies very seriously and expected that their contributions would be used to make a difference in the lives of other graduate students. To appropriately honor graduate students' involvement, assessors should consider how, if at all, the information will be used to improve graduate education. Individuals conducting assessment projects should be prepared to share those strategies with participants.

When Feasible, Share Resource Information. One striking outcome of these studies was the extent to which graduate students lacked awareness of the resources available to them. Students described a host of situations in which they needed information, ranging from student housing and health benefits to more complex issues such as conflicts with faculty advisors, harassment, and discrimination.

Individuals conducting assessment projects with graduate students should be knowledgeable about available campus and community resources. When it is feasible to do so (generally, after the interview has concluded so as not to influence the information shared by participants), facilitators should be prepared to provide accurate information about resources. Doing so constitutes one means of meeting the reciprocity expectations of qualitative research (Glesne, 2005). At all times, however, keep in mind that the primary relationship must be that of researcher, not problem solver.

Recognize the Limits of Your Assessment Methods and Results. Assessment projects have limitations that must be acknowledged. For instance, graduate students were not required to participate in the MSU or UM studies, thus begging the question, "Why did they come?" One could speculate that only individuals who were overly satisfied or dissatisfied chose to participate. Open invitation focus groups potentially skew results based on who does and does not attend. In these studies, focus groups offered investigators the opportunity to talk with greater numbers of students in fewer interview sessions. They also might have precluded participation by some graduate students who were uncomfortable with the group interview format, such as students whose first language is not English or students with disabilities. The usefulness of assessment results depends on an understanding and acknowledgment of the limitations of the methods used.

Recognize Assessment as a Service. Graduate students thanked us for allowing them the opportunity to express their views. They also commented on how helpful it was to talk with other graduate students. Because there are few structures in place that allow graduate students to meet other graduate students from different disciplines, the focus groups in the UM and MSU studies also served the purpose of connecting students with one another and providing a venue in which they could discuss their needs and experiences.

Conclusion

Assessing graduate students' needs and experiences represents a critical step in enhancing graduate education. In addition to general strategies offered by Schuh and Upcraft (1996, 2001), this chapter identified specific strategies for consideration in assessment involving graduate students. To assess the needs and experiences of graduate students, investigators should (1) consider issues of access and the timing of the study, (2) involve stakeholders, (3) pay attention to the political landscape of graduate education, (4) know the intended uses of the information, (5) share resource information when appropriate, (6) recognize and acknowledge limits of the assessment methods and results, and (7) recognize the potential of assessment as a service to graduate students.

Although research on graduate students provides general information about needs and experiences, assessment garners institution-specific data that can guide practices to best meet the needs of graduate students. In the three studies described in this chapter, for instance, graduate students noted (1) frustration with, and difficulty in, meeting the various professional and personal demands on their time and energy; (2) a lack of accommodation for the multiple roles they filled; (3) concerns about career plans and future employment opportunities; (4) a lack of opportunities to meet, learn from, and socialize with other graduate students; (5) the essential but volatile nature of relationships with faculty; and (6) a need for better communication and more information about available resources.

Lessons learned from these studies indicate the need for services and programs designed specifically for graduate students. The remaining chapters in this volume address means for improving graduate education. We begin with a discussion of the developmental trajectories of graduate students and a consideration of the educational and equity challenges for nontraditional graduate students. Outlines of specific program and service needs follow, including career planning and development services, graduate student centers, programs to foster professional ethics, and innovative programs of good practice.

NEW DIRECTIONS FOR STUDENT SERVICES • DOI: 10.1002/ss

References

Anderson, M. S., and Swazey, J. P. "Reflections on the Graduate Student Experience: An Overview." In M. S. Anderson (ed.), *The Experience of Being in Graduate School: An Exploration.* New Directions for Higher Education, no. 101. San Francisco: Jossey-Bass, 1998.

Austin, A. E. "Preparing the Next Generation of Faculty: Graduate School as Socialization to the Academic Career." *Journal of Higher Education,* 2002, 73(1), 94–122.

Baird, L. L. "The Melancholy of Anatomy: The Personal and Professional Development of Graduate and Professional Students." In J. C. Smart (ed.), *Higher Education: Handbook of Theory and Research.* New York: Agathon Press, 1990.

Baird, L. L. "Using Research and Theoretical Models of Graduate Student Progress." In L. J. Baird (ed.), *Increasing Graduate Student Retention and Degree Attainment.* New Directions for Institutional Research, no. 80. San Francisco: Jossey-Bass, 1993.

Banta, T. W. "A Call for Transformation." In T. W. Banta (ed.), *Building a Scholarship of Assessment.* San Francisco: Jossey-Bass, 2002.

Barker, S., Felstehausen, G., Couch, S., and Henry, J. "Orientation Programs for Older and Delayed-Entry Graduate Students." *NASPA Journal,* 1997, 35(1), 57–68.

Baxter Magolda, M. B. "Developing Self-Authorship in Graduate School." In M. S. Anderson (ed.), *The Experience of Being in Graduate School: An Exploration.* New Directions for Higher Education, no. 101. San Francisco: Jossey-Bass, 1998.

Bowen, W. G., and Rudenstine, N. L. *In Pursuit of the Ph.D.* Princeton, N.J.: Princeton University Press, 1992.

Boyle, P., and Boice, B. "Best Practices for Enculturation: Collegiality, Mentoring, and Structure." In M. S. Anderson (ed.), *The Experience of Being in Graduate School: An Exploration.* New Directions for Higher Education, no. 101. San Francisco: Jossey-Bass, 1998.

Conrad, C. F., Haworth, J. G., and Millar, S. B. *A Silent Success: Master's Education in the United States.* Baltimore, Md.: Johns Hopkins University Press, 1993.

Forney, D. S., and Davis, T. L. "Ongoing Transition Sessions for Student Affairs Master's Students." *Journal of College Student Development,* 2002, 43, 288–293.

Glesne, C. *Becoming Qualitative Researchers: An Introduction.* (3rd ed.) Needham Heights, Mass.: Allyn and Bacon, 2005.

Golde, C. M. "How Departmental Contextual Factors Shape Doctoral Attrition." Unpublished doctoral dissertation, Stanford University, 1996.

Golde, C. M. "Beginning Graduate School: Explaining First-Year Doctoral Attrition." In M. S. Anderson (ed.), *The Experience of Being in Graduate School: An Exploration.* New Directions for Higher Education, no. 101. San Francisco: Jossey-Bass, 1998.

Golde, C. M., and Dore, T. M. "At Cross Purposes: What the Experiences of Today's Doctoral Students Reveal About Doctoral Education." 2001. Retrieved Aug. 30, 2005, from http://www.phd-survey.org.

Group for the Advancement of Psychiatry. *Making the Grade: Helping Students Adapt to Graduate School.* New York: Haworth Press, 1999.

Haworth, J. G. (ed.). *Assessing Graduate and Professional Education: Current Realities, Future Prospects.* New Directions for Institutional Research, no. 96. San Francisco: Jossey-Bass, 1996.

Herman, D. A., and Hazler, R. J. "Adherence to a Wellness Model and Perceptions of Psychological Well-Being." *Journal of Counseling and Development,* 1999, 77, 339–343.

Hodgson, C. S., and Simoni, J. M. "Graduate Student Academic and Psychological Functioning." *Journal of College Student Development,* 1995, 36, 244–253.

Lee, J., and Graham, A. V. "Students' Perception of Medical School Stress and Their Evaluation of a Wellness Elective." *Medical Education,* 2001, 35, 652–659.

Lovitts, B. E. "Leaving the Ivory Tower: A Sociological Analysis of the Causes of Departure from Doctoral Study." Unpublished doctoral dissertation, University of Maryland, 1996.

Lovitts, B. E. *Leaving the Ivory Tower: The Causes and Consequences of Departure from Doctoral Study.* Lanham, Md.: Rowman and Littlefield, 2001.

Lovitts, B. E., and Nelson, C. "The Hidden Crisis in Graduate Education: Attrition from Ph.D. Programs." *Academe,* 2000, *86,* 44–50.

Marshall, C., and Rossman, G. B. *Designing Qualitative Research.* (3rd ed.) Thousand Oaks, Calif.: Sage, 1999.

Merriam, S. B. *Qualitative Research and Case Study Applications in Education.* San Francisco: Jossey-Bass, 1998.

Nerad, M., and Miller, D. S. "Increasing Student Retention in Graduate and Professional Programs." In J. Grant Haworth (ed.), *Assessing Graduate and Professional Education: Current Realities, Future Prospects.* New Directions for Institutional Research, no. 92. San Francisco: Jossey-Bass, 1996.

Nyquist, J. D., and others. "On the Road to Becoming a Professor." *Change,* 1999, *31*(3), 18–27.

Owen, T. R. "Self-Directed Learning Readiness Among Graduate Students: Implications for Orientation Programs." *Journal of College Student Development,* 1999, *40,* 739–743.

Palomba, C. A. "Implementing Effective Assessment." In C. A. Palomba and T. W. Banta (eds.), *Assessing Student Competence in Accredited Disciplines.* Sterling, Va.: Stylus, 2001.

Poock, M. C. "Graduate Student Orientation: Assessing Needs and Methods of Delivery." *Journal of College Student Development,* 2002, *43,* 231–244.

Poock, M. C. "Graduate Student Orientation Practices: Results from a National Survey." *NASPA Journal,* 2004, *41,* 470–486.

Pruitt-Logan, A. S., and Isaac, P. D. (eds.). *Student Services for the Changing Graduate Population.* New Directions for Student Services, no. 72. San Francisco: Jossey-Bass, 1995.

Schuh, J. H., and Upcraft, M. L. "Assessment Politics." *About Campus,* 2000, *5*(4), 14–21.

Schuh, J. H., and Upcraft, M. L. *Assessment Practice in Student Affairs: An Applications Manual.* San Francisco: Jossey-Bass, 2001.

Tinto, V. *Leaving College: Rethinking the Causes and Cures of Student Attrition.* (2nd ed.) Chicago: University of Chicago Press, 1994.

Upcraft, M. L., and Schuh, J. H. *Assessment in Student Affairs: A Guide for Practitioners.* San Francisco: Jossey-Bass, 1996.

Van Maanen, J., and Schein, E. H. "Toward a Theory of Organized Socialization." *Research in Organizational Behavior,* 1979, *1,* 209–264.

Weidman, J. C., Twale, D. J., and Stein, E. L. *Socialization of Graduate and Professional Students in Higher Education: A Perilous Passage.* ASHE-ERIC Higher Education Report, vol. 28, no. 3. San Francisco: Jossey-Bass, 2001.

BECKI ELKINS NESHEIM *is director of institutional research at Cornell College in Mt. Vernon, Iowa.*

MELANIE J. GUENTZEL *is director of graduate student services at St. Cloud State University and a doctoral candidate in student affairs administration and research at the University of Iowa.*

ANN M. GANSEMER-TOPF *is a research and assessment analyst at Grinnell College in Grinnell, Iowa.*

LEAH EWING ROSS *recently completed her doctorate in educational leadership and policy studies at Iowa State University.*

CATHRYN G. TURRENTINE *is in private practice as an assessment consultant.*

2

Student development theories offer frameworks for better understanding and enhancing the experiences of graduate and professional students.

Graduate and Professional Student Development and Student Affairs

Ann M. Gansemer-Topf, Leah Ewing Ross, R. M. Johnson

Historically, student affairs professionals have focused on the needs and development of undergraduate students. The research and theory associated with the development of college students is termed *student development theory*. This theory draws heavily on research conducted in psychology and sociology. The traditional focus of student affairs frames knowledge about and discussions on student development theory primarily within the context of undergraduate education (see, for instance, Evans, Forney, and Guido-DiBrito, 1998). Learning and development, however, occur across the life span, and many of these theoretical paradigms extend beyond the undergraduate environment and can be applied to students pursuing jgraduate and professional education (see Baxter Magolda, 1992; King and Kitchener, 1994; Perry, 1970; Schlossberg, 1995).

Student affairs professionals, as well as other educators, use student development theory to enhance undergraduate student involvement, persistence, and learning (see, for instance, Astin, 1993; Pascarella and Terenzini, 1991, 2005). Pontius and Harper (Chapter Four, this volume) provide an example of how the concept of engagement can be extended to provide the theoretical underpinning for services that meet the needs of graduate and professional students.

This chapter reviews relevant student development theories as they apply to graduate and professional students. We also make suggestions on

New Directions for Student Services, no. 115, Fall 2006 © Wiley Periodicals, Inc.
Published online in Wiley InterScience (www.interscience.wiley.com) • DOI: 10.1002/ss.213

how student affairs professionals can use this literature to enhance the educational experiences of these students.

Background and Context

Degree completion rates for graduate students vary. Some professional programs have completion rates of 90 percent, while as many as 50 percent of students who begin doctoral programs do not persist to graduation (Bowen and Rudenstine, 1992; Lovitts, 2001; Tinto, 1993). Since graduate work is a significant investment of time and money for students, faculty, and institutions (Smallwood, 2004), understanding why graduate students do not persist is valuable knowledge. Indeed, calls have been made for additional research to examine factors related to graduate and professional student persistence (Golde, 2000; Tinto, 1993).

A long-standing belief within the academy is that graduate student success is based primarily on students' academic abilities and aptitudes (Golde, 2000; Lovitts, 2001). As a result, many institutions have focused their attention on reexamining characteristics of the students they admit by implementing tougher admissions standards. However, Lovitts's study of doctoral students found that students' academic abilities were not the primary contributors to their lack of persistence. Rather, there were other aspects of students' emotional, social, and cognitive experiences that played more critical roles in student success. Social integration and peer relationships are particularly important (Lovitts, 2001; Tinto, 1993).

For educators trained to view student experiences holistically, this finding probably does not come as a surprise. Student affairs professionals, whose mission is to focus on the whole student, have developed programs and services to promote students' emotional, social, and cognitive development. While most of this work has focused on students pursuing undergraduate degrees, a similar approach can be taken to affect graduate students' experiences. It is not enough to evaluate student characteristics and backgrounds prior to admission into graduate and professional programs. More research needs to be conducted to understand the experiences of students while in such programs (Lovitts, 2001; Tinto, 1993).

This chapter focuses on student development theories as they relate to graduate and professional students. We recognize that discussing frameworks for graduate student development can be problematic because students enroll in graduate and professional programs at different ages and with different personal and professional experiences and responsibilities. Nevertheless, presenting some general information on graduate student development can benefit educators working with graduate students by providing a theoretical foundation for developing programs and services geared toward them. Before we address student development and specific interventions, however, it is important to look at the forces in graduate and professional education that affect the student experience.

Socialization in Graduate School

Graduate and professional education is frequently discussed as a process of socialization into the culture, values, and mores of a chosen profession. Weidman, Twale, and Stein (2001), drawing on literature from career development, adult socialization, and role acquisition, have developed a model for illustrating the socialization process in graduate school. They define graduate school socialization as "the processes through which individuals gain the knowledge, skills, and values necessary for successful entry into a professional career requiring the advanced level of specialized knowledge and skills" (p. iii).

The model proffered by Weidman, Twale, and Stein (2001) presents a dynamic and nonlinear view of graduate education, asserting that socialization occurs through the interaction among the stages of socialization (anticipatory, formal, informal, and personal), the core socialization experience (normative context, core socialization process, and core elements), and the contextual dimensions (prospective students, personal communities, professional communities, and novice professional practitioners). It provides a model of the complexity involved in socialization to a profession.

The socialization process proposed by Weidman, Twale, and Stein (2001) builds on the four stages of role acquisition identified by Thornton and Nardi (1975): anticipatory, formal, informal, and personal. The anticipatory stage occurs during the recruitment and admissions period as students begin to learn the expectations of the program and what it means to be a professional in a specific discipline. Prospective graduate and professional students often have preconceived ideas about what to expect from the academy (Golde and Dore, 2001). The experience during the anticipatory stage serves to either verify or alter these ideas (Weidman, Twale, and Stein, 2001). Little mutual interaction occurs in this stage; rather, prospective students are engaged in top-down relationships in which students are the receivers of information.

The second stage, the formal stage, begins when students are admitted to graduate programs and begin formal instruction. The expectations that were outlined in the prior stage (anticipatory) become clearer as they are applied directly to students. Students have a chance to practice their roles through their performance in course work and interactions with faculty and students (Weidman, Twale, and Stein, 2001). They rely less on the formal structures in graduate school to develop their roles and incorporate more of the informal aspects of graduate school during the third (informal) stage. They learn more about their roles through their expectations and appropriate behaviors with others. Faculty members are still critical at this stage, but the role of peers increasingly becomes important (Weidman, Twale, and Stein, 2001). Opportunities to interact in social settings or in less structured settings are important for this stage.

NEW DIRECTIONS FOR STUDENT SERVICES • DOI: 10.1002/ss

Finally, during the personal stage, students internalize the roles of the profession and establish a professional identity. However, during this time individuals might alter the roles and expectations to fit their needs and interests. For instance, they might take on research projects that match their interests separate from those of peers or advisors (Weidman, Twale, and Stein, 2001).

Although the socialization process stages are somewhat hierarchical, they are also interactive (Weidman, Twale, and Stein, 2001). For example, through course work, students might gain the technical knowledge needed for the profession (formal socialization) while also meeting with other graduate students to discuss research projects (informal socialization). In addition, one of the key success factors for graduate students can be found in sharing an office with other graduate students (Lovitts, 2001). An office provides a context in which students can interact as professionals, introducing new students to the departmental culture, while also providing personal support.

Within each of these stages, three core elements—knowledge acquisition, investment, and involvement—also influence socialization. Knowledge acquisition includes both the formal and informal knowledge needed to be successful. Technical knowledge and skills, history, culture, and the language of the profession are learned. Learning will also incorporate more affective knowledge and skills, such as understanding the expectations of the profession and assessing whether one has the ability to meet these expectations (Weidman, Twale, and Stein, 2001).

A second element, investment, includes a commitment of personal value, such as "time, alternative career choices, self-esteem, [and] social status" (Weidman, Twale, and Stein, 2001, p. 17). Assuming students make adequate progress in their degree programs, the level of investment increases the longer the students remain in the program. In the anticipatory stage, for instance, the level of investment includes committing to and enrolling in specific graduate programs. During the formal stage, students invest time and energy through taking courses. These levels of investment increase as students also become involved in research projects or work directly with one or more faculty members. It should also be noted that students vary in the level and intensity of their investments due to other factors (Weidman, Twale, and Stein, 2001). For example, individuals who quit their jobs and relocate to new institutions to become full-time students and graduate assistants might feel that they have made more significant investments than students who maintained their current positions and enrolled in graduate programs close to home.

Involvement, the third element, entails "participation in some aspect of the professional role or in preparation for it" (Weidman, Twale, and Stein, 2001, p. 18). Similar to investment, students vary in the intensity and frequency of their involvement. For some students, involvement includes what is defined by curricular requirements, such as course work and the dissertation. For others, involvement includes fulfilling degree requirements, but also undertaking other activities, such as research and teaching assistant-ships, independent research projects, presenting at conferences, and attend-ing professional meetings.

Similar to the stages, these three elements do not occur in isolation; they interact to either accelerate or slow progress to professional socialization (Weidman, Twale, and Stein, 2001). For instance, enrolling in a class provides students with specific knowledge about the profession while simultaneously requiring an investment in time and energy and involvement with faculty members and peers. Although not distinct, these elements play critical roles in how students learn about their professions, begin to be socialized into the roles of those professions, and ultimately assume professional identities.

Student affairs divisions can enrich the socialization processes of grad-uate and professional programs in a variety of ways. In the formal stage, for instance, student affairs professionals can collaborate with other academic units to coordinate a student orientation program that includes information about housing, counseling, and health services. By providing social events and activities geared toward graduate students or by supporting a graduate student government association, educators can encourage the needed infor-mal interaction among graduate and professional students. Adult develop-ment and student development theories currently in use by student affairs practitioners can provide a basis for developing programs and intervening in the socialization process.

Adult Development and Student Development Theories

Adult development theory, like student development theory, is based in research from psychology, sociology, and education. It encompasses student development theory and includes populations beyond traditional-aged college students. There are four primary theoretical approaches to adult development: life span perspective, developmental perspective, transition perspective, and contextual perspective (Schlossberg, Waters, and Good-man, 1995). Although they have distinct approaches to development, there is overlap among them. We examine three of these theoretical approaches here: life span, developmental, and transition. The fourth approach, the con-textual perspective, emphasizes the environment and social context in which development occurs. We believe this perspective is best captured by the dis-cussion of socialization above and thus do not repeat that discussion here.

Life Span Perspective. The life span perspective views adult develop-ment as a uniquely individual and variable process (Schlossberg, Waters, and Goodman, 1995). As such, life span theorists oppose stages of develop-ment that are more hierarchical, irreversible and cumulative. Instead, they believe that individuals are shaped by life events or milestones and that the significance of life events is influenced by individual experiences, culture, and gender (Brim and Kagan, 1980; Whitbourne, 1985). Viewed through this lens, it would be difficult to define a graduate student experience that would be relevant to everyone. The significance and impact of the graduate experience, rather, can be ascertained only by examining the characteristics and circumstances of the individual. This perspective is useful in reminding faculty members and student affairs professionals that although theories can be helpful in identifying potential difficulties or challenges, individual traits must also be considered. More frequently applied in the field of student affairs is the developmental perspective, to which we now turn.

Developmental Perspective. According to Schlossberg, Waters, and Goodman (1995), the developmental perspective views individuals as moving through specific stages and, according to Perry (1970), positions. These theories examine development from a variety of perspectives (for example, age, psychological, or cognitive), but they all assume that individuals progress in a sequential manner. Because graduate education constitutes an academic pursuit designed to stretch the mind, this section focuses on theories of cognitive development applicable to graduate and professional students.

Cognitive development—the processes and structures individuals use to make meaning of their worlds (Love and Guthrie, 1999)—plays a critical role in graduate students' successful degree completion. Graduate and professional students need to be able to analyze issues and problems while recognizing and appreciating multiple viewpoints and then select the best solution with supporting evidence. These abilities are representative of higher orders of processing information and constructing knowledge.

Love and Guthrie (1999) explored the cognitive development theories of Perry (1970), Baxter Magolda (1992), Belenky, Clinchy, Goldberger, and Tarule (1986), and King and Kitchener (1994). They identified three key common epistemological views among the theories: unequivocal knowing, radical subjectivity, and generative knowing. Although each theory presents different perspectives on each of the categories, there are common tenets among them.

In *unequivocal knowing,* "knowers view the world as having a single, universal truth" (Love and Guthrie, 1999, p. 77). This type of knowledge and truth cannot be challenged. Truth and knowledge are absolute and come from those who are in positions of authority and power. Truth is the same for all. In *radical subjectivism,* the certainty and authority experienced in unequivocal knowing begin to disintegrate. The knower moves to a world in which truth is uncertain and ambiguous, and all perspectives are equally valid and potential sources of truth (Love and Guthrie, 1999). This shift is continued in the "great accommodation," "when the individual comes to realize that uncertainty is neither anomalous nor restricted to certain knowledge domains—that it is evident everywhere" (p. 79).

The theories have less in common after the great accommodation, as each theorist explores the more complex stages of cognitive development in *generative knowing.* Each theory, however, offers a perspective of knowers' understanding their own agency in the knowing process. Furthermore, "though each theory varies considerably in methodologies used to examine epistemological beliefs and thinking, . . . [they] indicate that generative knowing would be rare at the undergraduate level but more common among graduate students" (Love and Guthrie, 1999, p. 80). Graduate and professional students with more life experience might be more likely to reach generative knowing than students who enter graduate school shortly after finishing their undergraduate degrees. Development depends on a student's willingness to grow, the challenges encountered, and the support provided.

To provide appropriate challenges and supports, it is important to assess students' cognitive development, specifically, whether students view knowledge from unequivocal knowing, radical subjectivity, or generative knowing perspectives. Love and Guthrie (1999) explained that "without the ability to assess students' levels of development, student affairs professionals will have only marginal success in understanding the students' perspective and encouraging their cognitive development" (p. 86). Supporting students' cognitive development is crucial for graduate and professional students because a higher order of knowing increases the potential for successfully completing terminal degree programs.

Equally important, and an area where student affairs practitioners can assert holistic views of students, is recognition of the impact of emotion, interpersonal relationships, and culture on cognitive development (Love and Guthrie, 1999). As Weidman, Twale, and Stein (2001) noted, socialization occurs through an individual's interaction with peers, faculty, and the environment. It affects the ways in which students acquire knowledge and the ways in which they experience graduate and professional education. Change and growth in one area of the self, such as cognitive development, affects students' interpersonal and psychosocial development as well. Attention to the developmental perspective necessitates tending to cognitive, psychosocial, interpersonal, and affective-emotional areas of personal growth and development.

The Transition Perspective. The transition to graduate or professional student can elicit feelings of self-doubt or new self-awareness and can change relationships with family or significant others. The emotional transition requires awareness and support. The transition perspective focuses on life events that bring about change (Schlossberg, Waters, and Goodman, 1995). These life-changing events can be anticipated, such as getting married or retiring, or unanticipated, such as the death of a loved one or the loss of a job. According to Schlossberg, Waters, and Goodman (1995) a transition is "any event, or non-event that results in changed relationships, routines, assumptions, and roles" (p. 27). The magnitude of the transitions required by graduate education varies among individuals, but few students can pursue graduate or professional education without experiencing some of the stress associated with transitions (Golde, 2000).

Three types of transitions exist: anticipated transitions, unanticipated transitions, and nonevents (Schlossberg, Waters, and Goodman, 1995). An anticipated transition is scheduled or predicted; an unanticipated transition is not predicted; a nonevent is something expected that does not occur. Enrolling in a professional program and the accompanying changes in lifestyle, work, or finances are a few of many anticipated transitions. A graduate student expecting to work as a research assistant who instead is given a last-minute teaching assistantship experiences an unanticipated event. A nonevent occurs, for example, when a graduate student who expects to lose her assistantship because of a lack of funding learns that funding has been secured and her assistantship will remain intact. In this case, an expected event, the loss of an assistantship, does not occur.

Context and impact also affect people's perceptions of transition. Context refers to the setting in which a transition takes place and the relationship of the individual to the event. Impact refers to the degree to which a transition alters daily life and includes the effects on relationships, routines, assumptions, and roles (Schlossberg, Waters, and Goodman, 1995). The context and impact of enrolling in graduate or professional programs can vary significantly for students. Some students make geographical moves to attend graduate school; for some students, graduate school means a strain on financial resources; other students begin graduate programs with significantly less disruption in their daily lives.

Individuals' perceptions of transition play a critical role in determining how stressful or significant transitions are. "A transition is not so much a matter of change as of the individual's own perception of the change" (Schlossberg, Waters, and Goodman, 1995, p. 28). A student who researched the institution, visited the department, and selected a program based on personal fit might find the transition less stressful than a student who selected a program based on prestige or geography. They might have enrolled in the same program at the same institution but react differently based on their expectations.

Schlossberg, Waters, and Goodman (1995) outlined four factors that influence people's abilities to cope with transition: situation, self, support, and strategies. The situation itself can influence coping. When is the transition occurring? Are there other transitions occurring at the same time? How much control does the individual have in the situation? A second factor is self. What are the personal characteristics and psychological resources of the individual? Support comprises a third factor. What other means of support do individuals have to help them deal with stress? Finally, what strategies can individuals employ to effectively modify or cope with transition?

These factors provide guidelines for student affairs professionals to begin to assess students' abilities to navigate transitions. We know, for example, that women and students of color are more likely to withdraw from doctoral programs than their white, male peers (Turner, Myers, and Creswell, 1999; Turner and Thompson, 1993). Women and students of color often cite isolation and lack of support as their reasons for withdrawal. What support systems are in place to overcome these issues, and what strategies can students use? Students of color who have strong support networks in the form of mentors or family might be less at risk of dropping out than their peers who lack such networks. Educators can develop a framework based on these four factors (situation, self, support, and strategies) to help identify potential contextual difficulties for students and develop appropriate institutional responses.

Roles for Student Affairs

In graduate education, typically the role of retaining and graduating students is the responsibility of individual departments (Weidman, Twale, and Stein, 2001). This emphasis is significantly different from the expectations of institutions regarding undergraduate education. At the undergraduate level, institutionwide programs such as orientation, first-year seminars, and learning communities exist to assist students in their transitions to college. The most effective of these programs require strong collaborations between academic affairs and student affairs. These same partnerships can be expanded to benefit graduate and professional students.

In Chapter One of this volume, Elkins Nesheim and others illustrate how student affairs professionals are in unique positions to evaluate the graduate school experience. Since graduate students might be hesitant to express their frustrations directly to academic departments for fear of retribution, student affairs professionals might be more likely to gain honest feedback. In addition, student affairs professionals can use their knowledge of student development theory to provide feedback and recommendations that align with the needs of graduate and professional students.

Polson (2003) describes a variety of ways in which student affairs can collaborate with academic units and graduate offices. For instance, she recommended that graduate student orientation programs be expanded to include information on child care, counseling services, disability resources, and community information. In addition, Polson suggested that student services offices work with academic departments in the areas of learning styles and study skills. In initiating these services, student affairs professionals should incorporate the work of cognitive development theorists. A solid base in research will lend credibility to the suggested programmatic interventions, as will a clear plan to assess the outcomes.

Poock (2002) found that campuswide orientation activities, in addition to traditional department activities, provided valuable information for new graduate students. In these instances, student affairs professionals can lend their knowledge and expertise related to student development and learning in efforts to assist graduate and professional students. Orientation programs can be developed to address some of the transition issues for graduate students (Schlossberg, Waters, and Goodman, 1995) and to have a positive impact on students as they begin the formal stage of the socialization process (Weidman, Twale, and Stein, 2001).

NEW DIRECTIONS FOR STUDENT SERVICES • DOI: 10.1002/ss

Services designed to meet the needs of people of color and women also are critical for student success (Poock, 2002; Weidman, Twale, and Stein, 2001). Some existing services could easily be adapted to the needs of graduate and professional students. Women's centers and multicultural centers can provide safe places for graduate and professional students, regardless of their academic disciplines, to connect with one another and build communities of support. These centers, made cognizant of the transitions or socialization processes of graduate students, can tailor programs, activities, and services to address these issues. For instance, the informal stage of socialization can be addressed by having new students connect with upper-level graduate students or by simply providing safe places for peers to meet to discuss issues related to their graduate or professional experiences.

"Giving support to graduate students provides a unique opportunity for collaboration between units that have not always worked together" (Polson, 2003, p. 67). Because many graduate students are focused within their specific departments and not on the larger university, student affairs professionals can be most effective if they work in conjunction with graduate offices and academic units. Nevertheless, their knowledge of student development and expertise in connecting theory to practice is also necessary as departments work toward improving the educational experiences of their graduate and professional students.

Conclusion

Understanding the epistemological perspectives, the transitions that occur, and the context in which graduate students take on roles as students will provide student affairs professionals with a framework for promoting holistic graduate and professional student development. Graduate and professional students represent the future development of their professions. Doctoral students, in particular, represent the future of the academy. As we contemplate meeting the needs of an increasingly diverse undergraduate population, it behooves us to treat graduate students as whole persons and work with them to view the student experience holistically.

The theories discussed here comprise only a few of many theories used to explain adult development. These theories provide insight into graduate and professional students' experiences and suggest that the challenges in becoming successful graduate students require more than simple mastery of disciplinary materials. Adjusting to new environments; juggling multiple roles of student, teacher, and researcher; and attending to personal relationships can play significant roles in students' progress toward their degrees. While graduate and professional programs are organized in ways to promote and assess mastery of discipline, they might not be structured to attend effectively to the nonacademic needs of students. Student affairs professionals, with their knowledge of student development and their history of attending to the academic and nonacademic needs of undergraduate students, can play a significant role in enhancing the graduate student experience.

References

Astin, A. W. *What Matters in College? Four Critical Years Revisited.* San Francisco: Jossey-Bass, 1993.

Baxter Magolda, M. B. *Knowing and Reasoning in College: Gender Related Patterns in Students' Intellectual Development.* San Francisco: Jossey-Bass, 1992.

Belenky, M. F., Clinchy, B. M., Goldberger, N. R., and Tarule, J. M. *Women's Ways of Knowing: The Development of Self, Voice and Mind.* New York: Basic Books, 1986.

Bowen, W. G., and Rudenstine, N. L. *In Pursuit of the Ph.D.* Princeton, N.J.: Princeton University Press, 1992.

Brim, O. G., and Kagan, J. *Constancy and Change in Human Development.* Cambridge, Mass.: Harvard University Press, 1980.

Evans, N. J., Forney, D. S., and Guido-DiBrito, F. *Student Development in College: Theory, Research, and Practice.* San Francisco: Jossey-Bass, 1998.

Golde, C. M. "Should I Stay or Should I Go? Student Descriptions of the Doctoral Attrition Process." *Review of Higher Education,* 2000, 23(2), 199–227.

Golde, C. M., and Dore, T. M. *At Cross Purposes: What the Experiences of Today's Doctoral Students Reveal About Graduate Education.* Philadelphia: Pew Charitable Trusts, 2001. (ED 450 628)

King, P. M., and Kitchener, K. S. *Developing Reflective Judgment: Understanding and Promoting Intellectual Growth and Critical Thinking in Adolescents and Adults.* San Francisco: Jossey-Bass, 1994.

Love, P. G., and Guthrie, V. L. "Synthesis, Assessment, and Application." In P. G. Love and V. L. Guthrie (eds.), *Synthesis, Assessment and Application.* New Directions for Student Services, no. 88. San Francisco: Jossey-Bass, 1999.

Lovitts, B. E. *Leaving the Ivory Tower: The Causes and Consequences of Departure from Doctoral Study.* Lanham, Md.: Rowman and Littlefield, 2001.

Pascarella, E. T., and Terenzini, P. T. *How College Affects Students.* San Francisco: Jossey-Bass, 1991.

Pascarella, E. T., and Terenzini, P. T. *How College Affects Students: A Third Decade of Research.* San Francisco: Jossey-Bass, 2005.

Perry, W. G. *Forms of Intellectual and Ethical Development in the College Years: A Scheme.* New York: Holt, 1970.

Polson, C. J. "Adult Graduate Students Challenge Institutions to Change." In D. Kilgore and P. J. Rice (eds.), *Meeting the Needs of Adult Students.* New Directions for Student Services, no. 102. San Francisco: Jossey-Bass, 2003.

Poock, M. C. "Graduate Student Orientation: Assessing Needs and Methods of Delivery." *Journal of College Student Development,* 2002, 43, 231–244.

Schlossberg, N. K., Waters, E. B., and Goodman, J. *Counseling Adults in Transition.* (2nd ed.) New York: Springer, 1995.

Smallwood, S. "Doctor Dropout: High Attrition from Ph.D. Programs Is Sucking Away Time, Talent, and Money—and Breaking Some Hearts, Too." *Chronicle of Higher Education,* Jan. 16, 2004, p. A10.

Thornton, R., and Nardi, P. M. "The Dynamics of Role Acquisition." *Journal of Sociology,* 1975, 80(4), 870–885.

Tinto, V. *Leaving College: Rethinking the Causes and Cures of Student Attrition.* (2nd ed.) Chicago: University of Chicago Press, 1993.

Turner, C.S.V., Myers, S. L., Jr., and Creswell, J. W. "Exploring Underrepresentation: The Case of Faculty of Color in the Midwest." *Journal of Higher Education,* 1999, *70*(1), 27–59.

Turner, C.S.V., and Thompson, J. "Socializing Women Doctoral Students: Minority and Majority Experiences." *Review of Higher Education,* 1993, *16*(3), 355–370.

Weidman, J. C., Twale, D. J., and Stein, E. L. *Socialization of Graduate and Professional Students in Higher Education.* ASHE-ERIC Higher Education Report, vol. 28, no. 3. San Francisco: Jossey-Bass, 2001.

Whitbourne, S. "The Psychological Construction of the Life Span." In J. E. Birren and K. W. Schaie (eds.), *Handbook of the Psychology of Aging.* (2nd ed.) New York: Van Nostrand Reinhold, 1985.

ANN M. GANSEMER-TOPF *is a research and assessment analyst at Grinnell College in Grinnell, Iowa.*

LEAH EWING ROSS *recently completed her doctorate in educational leadership and policy studies at Iowa State University.*

R. M. JOHNSON *is a postdoctoral fellow at the Research Institute for Studies in Education at Iowa State University.*

With the significant increase in graduate students characterized as nontraditional, challenges associated with balance have become more prominent. The author explores issues of work-life balance, institutional ownership, and the chilly climate, each of which can contribute to negative academic outcomes.

Seeking Balance in Graduate School: A Realistic Expectation or a Dangerous Dilemma?

Chris Peterson Brus

Deciding to go back to school for a graduate degree after being in the workforce for many years is a daunting prospect and a decision not made lightly (Golde and Dore, 2001; Rovaris, 2004). I remember sitting in my unfinished basement taking practice tests for the Graduate Record Exam (GRE), trying to concentrate while half-listening to my two young daughters playing above me. I knew I would never get in, especially after the GRE math refresher course was canceled. It had been twenty years since I had taken a math course. But the terror of taking the GRE was nothing compared to the terror I felt when I received my acceptance letter.

I knew I was smart, very smart, but I was also very rusty, unused to using my brain in traditional academic ways. I also was keenly aware that not only was I old enough to be some of the other students' mother, I was a mother myself, with two young children, a neurotic dog, two aging parents, three jobs, a mortgage, and a marriage that was disintegrating. Was I nuts going back to school? Maybe, but I found I was in good company.

Graduate students often struggle to balance their academic pursuits with their personal lives and responsibilities. These groups, in particular, face challenges: women; students of color; students with physical or learning disabilities; lesbian, gay, bisexual, and transgendered students; older students; international students; and students caring for dependent minors or adults. This chapter explores their dilemmas in depth. I begin with a discussion of

New Directions for Student Services, no. 115, Fall 2006 © Wiley Periodicals, Inc.
Published online in Wiley InterScience (www.interscience.wiley.com) • DOI: 10.1002/ss.214

the shifting demographic characteristics of graduate students followed by a consideration of work-life balance for graduate students. I conclude by offering intervention strategies for helping graduate students, particularly nontraditional students, navigate the myriad academic and personal decisions they face.

Changing Characteristics of the Graduate Student Population

Data collected annually by the U.S. Department of Education, National Center for Education Statistics (NCES), reveal shifts in the demographic characteristics of graduate students over the past three decades, resulting in a more diverse and less traditional graduate student population than in the past. We can track these shifts by looking at trends in the subpopulations already noted and in select indicators (age and dependent status). Women continue to enroll in graduate programs in record numbers, increasing from only 39 percent of enrollees in 1970 to 58 percent in 2000 (U.S. Department of Education, 2003; American Council on Education, 2005). NCES also reports that while the number of full-time male graduate students increased by 17 percent between 1990 and 2000, the number of women attending graduate school full time increased by 57 percent (U.S. Department of Education, 2003). Students of color and international students also experienced increased representation in graduate schools, with U.S. minority student enrollment doubling from 10 percent to 20 percent between 1975 and 2001, a trend that was mirrored by international students, whose numbers increased from 6 percent to 13 percent over the same time span (U.S. Department of Education, 2003). Data from the National Science Foundation (2003) show that as of 2003, women represented 42 percent of the graduate enrollment in science, technology, engineering, and math (STEM) disciplines (up 5 percent from 2002). Similar increases from 2002 to 2003 were noted for African American (6 percent) and Hispanic (8 percent) graduate student enrollees. International students represented 31 percent of all STEM graduate students in 2003, a 1 percent decline from 2002.

Another shift away from the homogeneous portrait of the traditional graduate student, one with significant implications for student affairs professionals, is the increase in students registering for accommodation based on a recognized disability. This number rose from 3 percent in 1995 to 6 percent in 2000, with almost half of those students reporting a diagnosis consistent with a learning disability (U.S. Department of Education, 2003). Little is known about the number of learning disabled students previously enrolled in graduate school because of a lack of data. One might assume, however, that an increase in the availability and visibility of support services following the adoption of the Americans with Disabilities Act in 1990, coupled with the increased frequency at which learning disabilities are diagnosed, has led to a more encouraging environment for affected students.

NEW DIRECTIONS FOR STUDENT SERVICES • DOI: 10.1002/ss

Another important demographic trend is the increasing age of graduate students (Hansen and Kennedy, 1995; Wagner, 2002). Although the average age for completion of a doctoral degree is reported as thirty-three years (Mason and Goulden, 2002; Mason, 2004; Williams, 2003), more than 40 percent of doctoral students attending the University of Iowa in 2001 were over the age of thirty, with 10 percent of those falling in the forty-and-over age category (Brus, 2003).

While age itself might not seem to be a significant factor for graduate education, the increased responsibility for family, both physically and financially, that is associated with an older, less traditional graduate student can be. In recognition that issues of family will place increased pressure on both the affected students and the institutions they attend, there is greater interest in documenting the number of graduate students with primary responsibility for dependents, both minor and adult (American Association of University Professors, 2001; Brus, 2003; Polson, 2003). Golde and Dore (2004) found that 9.3 percent of graduate students they surveyed in chemistry and 16.8 percent of those in English reported having at least one dependent child. Data from the Graduate Programs Climate Study survey conducted at the University of Iowa in 2001 revealed that more than one in four doctoral students reported having at least one minor dependent, with 9 percent reporting major responsibility for at least one adult dependent. Furthermore, 5 percent of respondents reported primary responsibility for minor dependents and adult dependents concurrently (Brus, 2003).

The changing demographics of graduate students are reflected in the increasing proportion of students who do not fit the traditional profile (Williams, 2004). Table 3.1 outlines general attributes differentiating traditional and nontraditional students. Recognizing the diversity inherent in today's graduate student population by incorporating a lens that includes nontraditional students shifts our focus away from one normative population and allows us to view the entire spectrum of students pursuing graduate education. Doing so provides much needed visibility to those challenges faced by nontraditional graduate students and enhances awareness of the need for appropriate academic and social support to increase retention for all graduate students.

Exploring Issues of Work-Life Balance

As director of the Women in Science and Engineering (WISE) Program at the University of Iowa, I am cognizant of issues of institutional equity for women in general and women of color in STEM disciplines. Work-life balance, institutional ownership, and the chilly climate of academe represent areas of concern for graduate students. Many graduate students experience periodic difficulty coping with these issues, but they predominantly disadvantage women and women of color (American Association of University Professors, 2001; American Council on Education, 2005; Curtis, 2004; University of California, Berkeley, 2005; Williams, 2003; Younes and Asay, 1998).

New Directions for Student Services • DOI: 10.1002/ss

Table 3.1. Generalized Demographic Differences Between Traditional and Nontraditional Graduate Students

Traditional Graduate Students Normative Population	Nontraditional Graduate Students Nonnormative Population
• Twenty-two to thirty years old	• Over thirty years old
• Primarily Caucasian	• Often from underrepresented populations; may be based on race, ethnicity, or gender
• Primarily from families with higher socioeconomic status	• Often from families with lower socioeconomic status
• Single, partnered, or married students with no children	• Married or single-parent students with dependent children
• Parents provide financial and emotional support to the student	• Parents increasingly dependent on the student for financial and emotional support

• Fewer hours of paid work
  • Fewer general time constraints
    • More opportunity for social interaction
    • More personal time for recreation and relaxation
	• More hours of paid work
	  • Greater general time constraints
	    • Less opportunity for social interaction
	    • Less personal time for recreation and relaxation

• More academic flexibility
  • More time on campus
  • More visibility in academic department
  • More opportunities to network
  • More availability on short notice
  • Increased probability of being mentored
	• Less academic flexibility
	  • Less time on campus
	  • Less visibility in academic department
	  • Fewer opportunities to network
	  • Less availability on short notice
	  • Decreased probability of being mentored

• Primary obligation is to excel in school	• Primary responsibility is the welfare of their family

For the population I serve, issues of work-life balance are not only critical to successful completion of a graduate degree but also play a significant role in a woman's ability to remain competitive for important postdoctoral and tenure-track positions after graduation. Unfortunately for both the affected women and the institution, successfully entering the faculty ranks does not lessen the importance of the issues surrounding work-life balance. These issues have been shown to exert negative pressure on a woman's career trajectory through tenure (American Council on Education, 2005; Mason, 2004; Sonnert, 1995; Williams, 2000), especially as they relate to successfully balancing the tenure clock and the biological clock (Fogg, 2003; Ginorio, 1995; Mason and Goulden, 2002; Mason, 2004; Sullivan, Hollenshead, and Smith, 2004; Williams, 2004).

But what exactly do we mean by work-life balance? As academic and social support advocates, faculty, and administrators, we so frequently talk about the need for and the benefits of a balanced approach to life that an assumption is made that we share a common definition for the word balance. It is important to define *balance* because such a definition can influence students' abilities to make appropriate work-life decisions.

Determining an Appropriate Definition of Balance. The notion of balance evokes the image of the scales of justice, barely teetering on either side of true equilibrium. The *American Heritage Dictionary of the English Language* (2000) provides two definitions of balance: "a state of equilibrium or parity characterized by cancellation of all forces by equal opposing forces" and "the power or means to decide." The thought of balance as static, constant, or controlled does not have much relevance to the lives of anyone I know, particularly those in graduate school, where the physical, mental, and emotional terrain can be rugged. To this end, I propose to use the second definition as a more honest definition of balance within the graduate school experience. This definition speaks directly to the individual's right to choose and his or her subsequent responsibility for those choices.

The Decision-Making Process. Graduate students with primary responsibility for dependents, especially those heading single-adult households, can provide excellent examples that underscore the complex decision-making process that many nontraditional students face (American Association of University Women, 1999). I often hear scenarios like those that follow during sessions with women who approach me for assistance negotiating an inflexible academic environment. Imagine grappling with quandaries such as these: (1) staying home with a sick child and not getting paid because you have no sick or vacation benefits, (2) taking a child to work, (3) missing a rescheduled midterm review or taking a parent to a scheduled doctor's appointment, or (4) quickly taking a midterm and then leaving to meet family responsibilities before returning for an evening meeting with an advisor.

These situations are representative of those I frequently experienced as a graduate student parent and are fairly representative of students with family responsibilities. Each of these situations necessitates a decision—a prioritization of competing responses, each of which might be critical to school, family, work, or some combination thereof.

The burden of constant decision making, always weighing and prioritizing the alternatives for least negative impact, can yield significant anguish and guilt (Rayman and Brett, 1993; University of California, Berkeley, 2005; Younes and Asay, 1998). Regardless of the choice made, there is always something important that was not chosen. Students in such positions are acutely aware that the repercussions of each decision affects those around them, especially partners and children, and that each decision will likely result in both positive and negative consequences (Thom, 2001; Younes and Asay, 1998). In my experience and those reported by many of the graduate women I serve, the difficulty associated with decision making is found in the accumulated weight of repeating the process several times a day, every day, often for years.

Balance, Gender, and Ethnicity. If challenges associated with work-life balance are significantly more pronounced in some populations of graduate students than others, what does that mean in terms of outcomes? There is, then, a strong association between increased family responsibility and diminished academic success (Curtis, 2004; Fogg, 2003; Sullivan, Hollenshead, and Smith, 2004; University of California, Berkeley, 2005; Williams, 2004; Younes and Asay, 1998). This association is especially prominent for women and students of color (Kerber, 2005; Mason and Goulden, 2002; Wagner, 2002). Couple those findings with data that show attrition rates remain higher for women than those for men and that students of color continue to leave graduate programs in higher numbers than their white counterparts, and it becomes apparent that institutions of higher learning are not yet invested in identifying and controlling the disincentives that continue to drive women and students of color from graduate programs (Golde, 1998; Rayman and Brett, 1993; Smallwood, 2004).

Institutional Ownership. Inflexibility is one of the least recognized or acknowledged constraints on graduate students with dependents. One of the most commonly reported difficulties associated with balancing multiple responsibilities is that of time management (Brennan, 1996; Curtin, Blake, Cassagnau, 1997; Polson, 2003; Scholer, 1998). While juggling multiple roles would create difficulty with time management, the challenges facing students with dependents are unnecessarily compounded by a culture of institutional ownership that is pervasive in graduate schools. Institutional ownership is an unstated but closely held expectation that students who are truly committed to their fields of study will make themselves available to their professors and advisors at any time of day or night, on short notice, and without negotiation or complaint. This expectation often translates into the necessity of students' spending sixty to eighty contact hours per week in their department merely to remain competitive (Fogg, 2003; Kerber, 2005; Mason, 2004; Williams, 2000). Although this expectation seems entirely unreasonable and borderline absurd, it developed through a natural phenomenon.

Colleges and universities, like most other institutions, develop a culture over time. In the nineteenth and early twentieth centuries in the United States, the right to attend college, and especially graduate school, was essentially reserved for and restricted to white males of means (Ginorio, 1995; Kerber, 2005). This population of students generally did not have to work to support themselves and often had mothers, wives, or domestic workers to take on the responsibilities associated with home and family (American Association of University Professors, 2001; Finkel and Olswang, 1996). As a result, they had the freedom to dedicate their undivided time to their academic studies (Williams, 2003). Being responsive to requests from professors, mentors, and advisors, no matter how outrageous, was a good way for a student to elevate his visibility with faculty and receive special attention, and competition for attention became fierce. Faculty began to see this competition for attention, and the resulting labor pool, as beneficial for themselves as well as for their students, and institutional ownership was born.

Unfortunately, institutions of higher learning still reflect the culture that grew from educating a very homogeneous, very privileged student population (Curtis, 2004). The practice of rewarding institutional ownership and its use as a yardstick to measure commitment is alive and well even though the graduate school population today bears scant resemblance to that of a century ago.

Differences Lead to a Chilly Climate. Competing responsibilities have an impact on a student's ability to be available and responsive to the requests of professors and advisors. If availability and responsiveness are used as indicators of commitment and probable success in graduate school, it follows that the student who is encumbered by nonacademic responsibilities will become differently valued by the institution. Although not generally acknowledged by faculty and administrators, the inability of a graduate student to fulfill the unstated obligations associated with institutional ownership leads to subtle changes in treatment and lowered expectations (Hansen and Kennedy, 1995; Widnall, 1988). This shift in perception and the changes in treatment that result are an integral part of the chilly climate often cited by women in STEM disciplines and students of color as an impediment to successful completion of graduate school (Ginorio, 1995; Thom, 2001). Far from being an overt form of discrimination, the chilly climate is a continuous loop of subtle reinforcement for negative stereotypes often assigned to students, especially those in underrepresented populations who have family responsibilities and increased time constraints (Moody, 2005; Widnall, 1988). While the insults that result from a chilly climate are most often small, unintentional, and difficult to identify as discriminatory, they are continuous and unrelenting, thereby sending a powerful message to those affected: if you are not part of the normative culture, you lack what it takes to be successful in graduate school (American Council on Education, 2005; Hansen and Kennedy, 1995; Kerber, 2005; Moody, 2005; Manz and Rossman, 2002; Widnall, 1988). This concept is illustrated in Figure 3.1.

A student can jump into the loop of negative consequences at virtually any point. Inability to fulfill the expectations of institutional ownership leads to a perceived lack of commitment, which leads to lowered expectations, which leads to less investment by faculty, which leads to fewer incentives and opportunities to excel, which leads to isolation and marginalization of affected students, which leaves them less competitive, less involved, and less likely to succeed (Widnall, 1988). The question becomes how we transform an obsolete institutional culture and break this destructive cycle.

Facilitating a Change in Institutional Culture

Four stakeholder groups have a part to play in initiating and sustaining an effort to advance a change in institutional culture: the institution as an entity (represented by upper administration), faculty and administrators at the department level, student affairs professionals and other academic and social support units, and graduate students (Hansen and Kennedy, 1995).

NEW DIRECTIONS FOR STUDENT SERVICES • DOI: 10.1002/ss

Figure 3.1. Circular Reinforcement of Negative Stereotypes Often Assigned to Nontraditional Students, Especially Those with Primary Responsibility for Children or Other Dependents

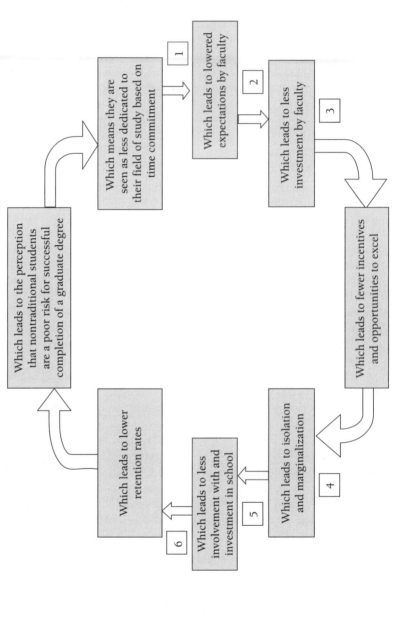

The institution itself must publicly acknowledge that issues of work-life balance, institutional ownership, and the chilly climate are issues of equity that, left unchallenged, can result in discriminatory practice (American Association of University Professors, 2001; American Council on Education, 2005; Euben, 2005; Hurtado, Milem, Clayton-Pederson, and Allen, 1998). If the institution espouses a commitment to diversity and underscores the importance of an inclusive academic community, it must respond specifically and forcefully to those institutional practices that disadvantage students (Fogg, 2003). Without visibility and support from senior administrators, there is little incentive to change long-standing policies and practices at the departmental level.

Breaking the Cycle of Negative Consequences Resulting from the Chilly Climate

Although the cycle presented in Figure 3.1 appears as a closed loop, there are points at which interventions might be successful in keeping at-risk students from either entering the loop or becoming hopelessly trapped there. The following recommendations offer to faculty, student affairs professionals, and graduate students general opportunities for intervention strategies that can be implemented as described or adapted to fit specific contexts and situations.

Intervention Point 1. This first intervention is to prevent a decrease in faculty expectations for graduate students who might appear less committed because increased family responsibilities limit their on-campus interactions and visibility (Widnall, 1988).

At the departmental level, advisors should be encouraged to schedule more frequent meetings with advisees they do not routinely see or interact with outside class, in the lab, or as part of required advising sessions. Scheduling additional meetings instead of leaving them to chance allows the student with severe time constraints to plan ahead and ensure his or her availability. This lessens the chance that a student will be penalized for decreased opportunities to interact informally with an advisor. It improves an advisor's ability early in the cycle to assess more accurately a student's commitment to graduate school and ensures increased opportunity for early identification of challenges that might be a threat to the student's commitment. Appropriate intervention can then be provided.

Student affairs providers should be integrated into existing departmental committees where issues of advising and academic support are routinely discussed. By increasing the frequency of interaction between faculty and student affairs professionals, both parties have the opportunity to learn how they benefit from working together (Boyle and Boice, 1998; Polson, 2003).

Student affairs professionals could engage faculty members in discussions about the availability and delivery of support services, resource information about student issues, guidelines for accessing appropriate support, and development of strategies for identifying students struggling to achieve work-life balance. A seamless provision of services to graduate students could result.

Graduate students who are unable to spend nonclass time on campus need to be creative and assertive in finding ways to stay in frequent contact with their advisors (Ellis, 2001; Rovaris, 2004). E-mail can be an important mechanism for increasing the interaction between graduate student women and their advisors since men report meeting with their advisors more often than do women (Widnall, 1988). This finding was supported by the University of Iowa Climate Survey that showed that men were more likely than women to meet with their dissertation advisors more than five times per semester, while women were more likely to report meeting with their dissertation advisors two or fewer times per semester (Brus, 2003). At a minimum, students should make contact with their advisors several times during a semester, even if there is no pressing issue to be addressed. This demonstrates a student's commitment to academic progress and success.

Intervention Point 2. Here the goal is to increase faculty investment in the academic success of nontraditional students.

At the departmental level, faculty must invest in the academic success of all graduate students, including nontraditional students, by helping students present their work. This can be done by strictly monitoring internal funds for travel to support all graduate students' attendance and presentations at professional meetings. Without a reasonable expectation that travel funds will be available, nontraditional students might not pursue opportunities to present posters or papers of their work at professional meetings, thereby enabling nontraditional students to remain academically competitive. In addition, advisors can provide entrée into a professional network and should consider attending at least one professional meeting with each of their advisees.

Student affairs professionals can be instrumental in furthering graduate students' professional development by offering programs that provide instruction in the preparation of a scientific poster or the development of a computer-based presentation. Career services staff, for instance, could partner with informational technology service providers to offer workshops on developing professional presentations. Academic departments and student affairs divisions could also partner to provide opportunities for graduate students to present their work to on-campus audiences. A positive experience giving a formal presentation to a campus-based group can decrease the fear of presenting at an academic conference.

Generally graduate students must learn to be their own advocates (Golde and Dore, 2001; Moody, 2005). If advisors are not supporting their advisees in a manner that is comfortable or productive, students should approach faculty, staff, or others in the department who might be helpful. Students could identify individuals within the department or another related department with whom they share common characteristics, such as family or dependent status, gender, race, ethnicity, or nationality (Ellis, 2001; Ginorio, 1995;

Moody, 2005). These individuals might be able to describe specific strategies they have employed to deal with challenges in graduate school similar to those that students may be facing. Often the key to success in graduate school, especially for nontraditional students, is less related to academic challenges than it is to surviving difficulties that arise in primary relationships. Graduate students would also do well to identify and use support services provided by student affairs offices and student organizations.

Intervention Point 3. Increasing the potential for nontraditional graduate students to excel by gaining leadership experience is the goal of this intervention.

At the departmental level, when a leadership opportunity arises, faculty should make the opportunity known to all graduate students and invite nominations, including self-nominations, for the position. Faculty should be open to candidates' listing references that are outside the institution and should avoid making judgments about the nominees' suitability or availability for a leadership experience based on characteristics that identify them as nontraditional (Euben, 2005). Faculty should seek input from faculty of color and other underrepresented constituents on how best to encourage the participation of nontraditional students as well as how best to accommodate their full participation.

Student affairs providers can assist all students, especially nontraditional students, who have not mastered the skills for developing a professional résumé, preparing a cover letter or letter of nomination, and identifying appropriate references. Leadership development programs tailored specifically to meet the needs of graduate students with a broad range of leadership styles could also prove fruitful.

Graduate students, especially those with multiple responsibilities, need to keep in mind that almost everything is negotiable (Babcock and Laschever, 2003; Evans, 2000). If a graduate assistantship is posted that would be perfect or departmental leadership opportunities are available, students must not assume they are out of the running and neglect to apply if the work hours listed are not compatible with child care or other obligations. If selected to interview, the student can ask if the work hours listed in the position description are open to negotiation. It is important for the student to approach the negotiation without apologizing for outside commitments. Expressing guilt about the need to accommodate family obligations serves to reinforce the value placed on institutional ownership. Simply submitting an application can alert faculty to the student's interest in pursuing leadership positions.

Intervention Point 4. Decreasing the isolation and marginalization of nontraditional graduate students is the next goal.

At the departmental level, faculty should require projects that involve working in small groups in all introductory and core courses (Treisman, 1992). Working in small groups during regularly scheduled classes the first two semesters of the graduate experience helps decrease the effect of isolation on students from underrepresented populations, promotes early formation of community within each incoming group of students, and increases the opportunities for interaction between traditional and nontraditional students (Sandler, Silverberg, and Hall, 1996).

Student affairs professionals can provide organizational and programmatic support for activities identified as important to incoming graduate students by including a short survey in each orientation packet that requests information in three categories: (1) basic demographic information about the student; (2) identification of types of academic support the student is interested in, such as study groups, tutoring services, job shadowing opportunities, and cooperative child care networks; and (3) a checklist of cultural, spiritual, recreational, intellectual, and political interests and activities. Student affairs staff can then provide organizational structure and coordination support to create networks of students based on the information submitted. The information should also be used to inform the development and provision of academic support services.

Graduate students must take advantage of opportunities to introduce themselves to other students in their classes and departments. Even students with the most severe time constraints can make contact with other students during the few minutes before class and can sit in class next to an acquaintance. In addition, students can network with other students, especially those who are in similar family situations. Building networks and communities with other graduate students can be one of the best ways to find support in navigating the demands of graduate school.

Intervention Point 5. Increasing involvement with and investment in school is the goal of this intervention.

At the departmental level, faculty can begin each academic year with a series of informal welcome events that occur on different days and at different times to encourage maximum overall participation. Departments can promote community building by sponsoring events open not only to faculty and students but to their families as well. The more opportunities the department sponsors that contribute to the development of a friendly, inclusive climate, not just among the students themselves but within the larger context of students and their families, the more invested students will become in their departments.

Student affairs professionals should partner with academic units to provide entering graduate students access to a broad range of information about programs designed to support their academic and social development. Information about child care, housing options, career development, writing seminars, and student organizations, for example, could be distributed during campus visit days and welcome events.

Graduate students must be cognizant of and diligent about taking advantage of the resources available to help make the transition into graduate school as easy and welcoming as possible. Institutions typically host a variety of events early in the academic year that are meant to assist in community building and identification of resources and that provide opportunities to meet staff, faculty, and other graduate students. As the intended recipients of all the planning, students have only one responsibility: to show up.

Intervention Point 6. All roads lead to retention.

In actuality, this intervention point serves not as a point of programmatic activity but as a sentinel for measuring institutional progress in evaluating how effectively we have managed issues of work-life balance, institutional ownership, and the chilly climate for graduate students. If, as suggested by Polson (2003), the steady increase in student enrollees categorized as nontraditional has and will continue to place pressure on institutions to provide a broader array of support services, it becomes imperative to recognize that the one-size-fits-all educational model informing institutional cultures today is no longer valid. Institutions of higher learning that respond to the needs of a diverse graduate student population will be those institutions that successfully increase retention rates, through graduation, for nontraditional graduate students (Golde, 1998; Weidman, Twale, and Stein, 2001).

Retention remains the one absolute measure of a student's successful navigation through the challenges of graduate school. It also measures the cumulative impact of many successful intervention and support services provided by the institution.

Conclusion

Looking back at my graduate school experience, I know that I often felt trapped between academic and family responsibilities, isolated, out of place, and different, not because anyone made a point to tell me I was different but because they did not have to. Through strategic interventions, faculty, student affairs professionals, and graduate students themselves can counter this phenomenon and foster appropriate work-life balance decisions.

References

American Association of University Professors. "Statement of Principles on Family Responsibilities and Academic Work." 2001. Retrieved Aug. 16, 2005, from http://www.aaup.org/statements/REPORTS/html.

American Association of University Women. "Gaining a Foothold: Women's Transitions Through Work and College." 1999. Retrieved May 8, 2005, from http://www.aauw.org/research/transitions.html. (ED 43 45 69)

American Council on Education. "An Agenda for Excellence: Creating Flexibility in Tenure-Track Faculty Careers." In *Executive Summary*. Washington, D.C.: American Council on Education, 2005.

The American Heritage Dictionary of the English Language, Fourth Edition. Boston: Houghton Mifflin, 2000. Retrieved Feb. 4, 2006, from http://www.bartleby.com/61/.

Babcock, L., and Laschever, S. *Women Don't Ask: Negotiation and the Gender Divide.* Princeton, N.J.: Princeton University Press, 2003.

Boyle, P., and Boice, B. "Best Practices for Enculturation: Collegiality, Mentoring, and Structure." In M. S. Anderson (ed.), *The Experience of Being in Graduate School: An Exploration.* New Directions for Higher Education, no. 101. San Francisco: Jossey-Bass, 1998.

Brennan, M. B. "Women Chemists Reconsidering Careers at Research Universities." *Chemical Engineering News*, 1996, *74*, 8–15.

Brus, C. P. "The University of Iowa Graduate Programs Climate Study: Doctoral Student Descriptive Data, Executive Summary." Iowa City: University of Iowa, Spring 2003.

Curtin, J. M., Blake, G., and Cassagnau, C. "The Climate for Women Graduate Students in Physics." *Journal of Women and Minorities in Science and Engineering*, 1997, *3*, 95–117.

Curtis, J. W. "Balancing Work and Family for Faculty: Why It's Important." *Academe Online*, 2004, *90*(6). Retrieved June 10, 2005, from http://www.aaup.org/publications/Academe.

Ellis, E. M. "The Impact of Race and Gender on Graduate School Socialization, Satisfaction with Doctoral Study, and Commitment to Degree Completion." *Western Journal of Black Studies*, 2001, *25*(1), 30–45, 2001.

Euben, D. "A Case to Consider: Working Mothers and Gender Discrimination." *Chronicle of Higher Education*, May 27, 2005, p. B12.

Evans, G. *Play Like a Man, Win Like a Woman: What Men Know About Success That Women Need to Learn.* New York: Broadway Books, 2000.

Finkel, S. K., and Olswang, S. G. "Child Rearing as a Career Impediment to Women Assistant Professors." *Review of Higher Education*, 1996, *19*(2), 123–139.

Fogg, P. "Family Time: Why Some Women Quit Their Coveted Tenure-Track Jobs." *Chronicle of Higher Education*, June 13, 2003, p. A10.

Ginorio, A. B. "Warming the Climate for Women in Academic Science." *Graduate Experience*, 1995, *23*, 12–14.

Golde, C. M. "Beginning Graduate School: Explaining First Year Doctoral Attrition." In M. S. Anderson (ed.), *The Experience of Being in Graduate School: An Exploration.* New Directions for Higher Education, no. 101. San Francisco: Jossey-Bass, 1998.

Golde, C. M., and Dore, T. M. "At Cross Purposes: What the Experiences of Today's Doctoral Students Reveal About Doctoral Education." Philadelphia: Pew Charitable Trusts, 2001. Retrieved July 16, 2005, from http://phd-survey.org/advice/advice.htm.

Golde, C. M., and Dore, T. M. "The Survey of Doctoral Education and Career Preparation. The Importance of Disciplinary Contexts." In D. H. Wulff and A. E. Austin (eds.), *Paths to the Professoriate: Strategies for Enriching the Preparation of Future Faculty.* Hoboken, N.J.: Wiley, 2004.

Hansen, E., and Kennedy, S. "Facing the Future, Surviving the Present: Strategies for Women." *Journal of Geography in Higher Education*, 1995, *19*(3), 307–315.

Hurtado, S., Milem, J. F., Clayton-Pederson, A. R., and Allen, W. R. "Enhancing Campus Climates for Racial/Ethnic Diversity: Educational Policy and Practice." *Review of Higher Education*, 1998, *21*, 279–302.

Kerber, L. K. "We Must Make the Academic Workplace More Humane and Equitable." *Chronicle of Higher Education*, Mar. 2005, p. B6.

Manz, H., and Rossman, G. "Promoting Women." *EMBO Reports*, 2002, *3*(1), 5–8.

Mason, M. A. "Do Babies Matter (Part II)? Closing the Baby Gap." *Academe*, 2004, *90*(6).

Mason, M. A., and Goulden, M. "Do Babies Matter? The Effect of Family Formation on the Lifelong Careers of Academic Men and Women." *Academe*, 2002, *88*(6), 21–27.

Moody, J. "Vital Info for Women and Underrepresented Graduate Students," San Diego, Calif.: J. Moody, 2005.

National Science Foundation. *Science and Engineering Indicators: 2000.* Washington, D.C.: National Science Foundation, Fall 2003.

Polson, C. J. "Adult Graduate Students Challenge Institutions to Change." In D. Kilgore and P. J. Rice (eds.), *Meeting the Needs of Adult Students.* New Directions for Student Services, no. 102. San Francisco: Jossey-Bass, 2003.

Rayman, P., and Brett, B. *The Graduate and Early Career Years.* Wellesley, Mass.: Center for Research on Women, 1993.

Rovaris Sr., D. J. "How to Successfully Manage the Graduate School Process." *Black Collegian*, 2004, *35*, 116–122.

Sandler, B. R., Silverberg, L. A., and Hall, R. M. *The Chilly Classroom Climate: A Guide to Improve the Education of Women.* Washington, D.C.: National Association for Women in Education, 1996.

Scholer, A. "Issues of Gender and Personal Life for Women in Academic Biology." *Journal of Women and Minorities in Science and Engineering,* 1998, *4,* 69–89.

Smallwood, S. "Doctor Dropout: High Attrition from Ph.D. Programs Is Sucking Away Time, Talent, and Money—and Breaking Some Hearts, Too." *Chronicle of Higher Education,* Jan. 16, 2004, p. A10.

Sonnert, G. "Gender Equity in Science: Still an Elusive Goal." *Issues in Science and Technology,* 1995, *12,* 53–58.

Sullivan, B., Hollenshead, C., and Smith, G. "Developing and Implementing Work-Family Policies for Faculty: Balancing Faculty Careers and Family Work." *Academe Online,* 2004, *90*(6). Retrieved June 10, 2005, from http://www.aaup.org/publications/Academe.

Thom, M. *Balancing the Equation: Where Are Women and Girls in Science, Engineering and Technology?* New York: National Council for Research on Women, 2001.

Treisman, U. "Studying Students Studying Calculus: A Look at the Lives of Minority Mathematics Students in College." *College Mathematics Journal,* 1992, *23,* 362–372.

University of California, Berkeley. "Faculty Family Friendly Edge: An Initiative for Tenure-Track Faculty at the University of California." Berkeley: University of California, Berkeley, Feb. 2005. Retrieved May 5, 2005, from http://ucfamilyedge.berkeley.edu/leaks.html.

U.S. Department of Education. National Center for Education Statistics. *Digest of Education Statistics.* Washington, D.C.: U.S. Department of Education, 2003.

Wagner, J. G. *Teaching the Growing Population of Nontraditional Students.* Reston, Va.: National Business Education Association, Nov. 2002. (ED 470 799)

Weidman, J. C., Twale, D. J., and Leahy Stein, E. *Socialization of Graduate and Professional Students in Higher Education. A Perilous Passage?* ASHE-ERIC Higher Education Report, vol. 28, no. 3. San Francisco: Jossey-Bass, 2001. (ED 457 710)

Widnall, S. E. "Voices from the Pipeline." *Science,* 1988, n.s. 241, 1740–1745.

Williams, J. C. "How the Tenure Track Discriminates Against Women." *Chronicle of Higher Education,* Oct. 27, 2000. Retrieved June 10, 2005, from http://chronicle.com/jobs/2000/10/2000102703c.htm.

Williams, J. C. "The Subtle Side of Discrimination." *Chronicle of Higher Education,* Apr. 18, 2003, p. C5. Retrieved June 10, 2005, from http://chronicle.com/weekly/v49/i32/32c00501.htm.

Williams, J. C. "Singing the Baby Blues." *Chronicle of Higher Education,* Apr. 23, 2004, p. C2. Retrieved Sept. 17, 2005, from http://chronicle.com/weekly/v50/i33/33c00201.htm.

Younes, M. N., and Asay, S. M. "Resilient Women: How Female Graduate Students Negotiate Their Multiple Roles." *College Student Journal,* 1998, *32,* 451–462.

CHRIS PETERSON BRUS *is director of Women in Science and Engineering at the University of Iowa.*

Student engagement represents a critical benchmark of educational effectiveness for graduate as well as undergraduate students. This chapter presents seven principles for good practice in engaging and connecting graduate and professional students to the larger campus community and provides examples of exemplary programs.

Principles for Good Practice in Graduate and Professional Student Engagement

Jason L. Pontius, Shaun R. Harper

Since the introduction of the National Survey of Student Engagement in 2000, faculty and administrators have devoted increased attention to determining the extent that students are engaged in educationally purposeful activities, both inside and outside the classroom. Subsequently, student engagement data have been used to rethink institutional practices and priorities, benchmark educational effectiveness among peer institutions, broaden public perceptions of collegiate quality, and ultimately improve undergraduate education and student learning (National Survey of Student Engagement, 2004). Kuh (2001) suggested that student engagement is a measure of institutional quality. Therefore, the more engaged that students are, the better the institution is. Similarly, Pascarella (2001) asserted, "An excellent undergraduate education is most likely to occur at those colleges and universities that maximize good practices and enhance students' academic and social engagement" (p. 22). Furthermore, Pascarella noted that several individuals and institutions have launched initiatives to identify excellence in education in response to public calls for accountability in higher education. Although graduate and professional students were 13.9 percent of all students enrolled in U.S. colleges and universities in 2001 (U.S. Department of Education, 2004), conversations and subsequent efforts to achieve educational excellence regarding student engagement have focused almost exclusively on undergraduates.

New Directions for Student Services, no. 115, Fall 2006   © Wiley Periodicals, Inc.
Published online in Wiley InterScience (www.interscience.wiley.com) • DOI: 10.1002/ss.215

In this chapter, we maintain that a parallel commitment should be made to identify excellence in graduate education. To this end, we offer a set of principles for good practice in graduate student engagement to serve as standards by which institutional effectiveness can be measured. We begin by considering the effects of misperceptions regarding the needs of graduate and professional students, as well as persistence trends among this population. The focus then shifts to introducing two sets of preexisting principles for good practice in undergraduate education and student affairs that served as models in the development of our principles. Following a brief synthesis of existing published evidence on the gains and outcomes associated with student engagement, we present seven principles for good practice in graduate education.

Misperceptions and Persistence Trends

Many postbaccalaureate degree programs, academic departments, and graduate and professional schools offer various services and resources for students. However, divisions of student affairs, especially those at large research universities, typically focus on undergraduate students, and hence devote less effort to engaging the graduate and professional student population. This trend is best explained by four factors: (1) undergraduate student enrollments often exceed those of graduate and professional students, (2) undergraduate student development arguably requires more attention and resources, (3) there is a belief that academic programs and departments already meet the needs of graduate students, and (4) the assumption is that graduate students, having experienced higher education as undergraduates, understand how to navigate institutional bureaucracies, thus warranting less attention than current undergraduates (Fischer and Zigmond, 1998).

These misperceptions and assumptions conceal several important issues. First, actual numbers of graduate students can be substantial, even if relative percentages are low in comparison to undergraduate enrollments. For instance, the University of Florida enrolled 14,299 graduate and professional students in 2004 (U.S. Department of Education, 2005). Although graduate students represented less than one-third of the total student body, they were a sizable population that likely needed specialized engagement efforts that should not be overlooked. This point is especially salient for institutions like Stanford University, Massachusetts Institute of Technology, and Harvard University, which enroll more graduate and professional students than undergraduates (U.S. Department of Education, 2005).

Another often neglected issue is that graduate students have specific needs and face developmental challenges that may differ from, but are as important as, those experienced by undergraduates. While many academic departments provide some support for graduate students, they often suffer from a building-bound silo effect that isolates them from the larger university. Academic units usually lack the human resources to adequately address many basic issues such as housing, counseling and wellness, and career development, let alone sponsor opportunities for engagement in educationally purposeful activities that reach beyond the department.

Finally, previous experience in higher education does not translate to graduate and professional experiences because of differences in graduate and undergraduate education, as well as variations in institutional types (Hartnett and Katz, 1977; Jorgenson-Earp and Staton, 1993; Lovitts, 2001; Pruitt-Logan and Isaac, 1995). For instance, an alumna from Spelman College, which enrolls 2,186 students (U.S. Department of Education, 2005), will likely find the Ohio State University quite different from and more challenging to navigate than her undergraduate institution. It would be misguided to conclude that support services and engagement efforts are unnecessary for this graduate student simply because she previously attended another postsecondary educational institution.

Recent examinations of doctoral student attrition have emphasized the roles that student affairs divisions can play in better supporting graduate and professional students (Council of Graduate Schools, 2004; Golde, 2000; Lovitts, 2001). While master's degree seekers, especially those in professional schools, tend to have higher retention rates, approximately 50 percent of doctoral students nationally leave their institutions before earning their degrees (Bowen and Rudenstine, 1992; Golde, 2000; Lovitts, 2001; National Research Council, 1996). Not only do schools lose talented and qualified students, they also forfeit enormous amounts of time and money invested in students through assistantships, fellowships, and professional development initiatives (Anderson and Swazey, 1998; Etzowitz, Kemelgor, Neuschatz, and Uzzi, 1992; Smallwood, 2004). Why does this level of attrition exist among doctoral students who, in theory, represent the best and brightest students on university campuses?

Contrary to the popular belief that academically ill-prepared students are weeded out, no correlation has been found between attrition and Graduate Record Exam scores, undergraduate grade point averages, and previous institutions from which bachelor's degrees were earned (Bair and Haworth, 1999; Golde, 1998; Lovitts, 2001). However, prior socialization to graduate school, student-faculty advising relationships, student engagement, and peer interaction correlate positively with persistence to degree. Lovitts (2001) found that students who received teaching assistantships were two times more likely, and those with research assistantships were almost three times more likely, to persist through degree attainment than were students who received fellowships. Lovitts attributed the difference to socialization and engagement: research assistants and teaching assistants work with and share office space with peers and have more opportunities for meaningful interactions with faculty and staff than do fellowship recipients. Astin (1993) found similar persistence trends for undergraduates who work part time on campus.

The effects of student engagement and socialization on graduate student persistence suggest that student affairs professionals can, and should, play significant roles in supporting and reaching out to graduate students.

While departments can provide clearer performance expectations and appropriate academic advising (Boyle and Boice, 1998; Council of Graduate Schools, 2004; Nerad and Miller, 1996), student affairs divisions should offer timely information and relevant campus services, and collaborate with departments to create supportive communities for graduate and professional students. Such efforts have proven effective in creating and sustaining excellence in undergraduate education.

Preexisting Models of Good Practices

Two widely read documents served as models for the principles presented later in this chapter. First, Chickering and Gamson's "Seven Principles for Good Practice in Undergraduate Education" (1987) offered a framework for institutional improvement based on years of evidence regarding educational effectiveness. The authors noted that the principles "rest on 50 years of research on the way teachers teach and students learn, how students work and play with one another, and how students and faculty talk to each other" (p. 3). Chickering and Gamson's seven principles have since guided student engagement dialogue, research, and practice. In fact, Kuh (1997) posited that the list of principles "is one of the most widely disseminated documents in American higher education" (p. 72).

Chickering and Gamson maintained that good practice in undergraduate education entails the following:

1. Encourages contact between students and faculty
2. Develops reciprocity and cooperation among students
3. Encourages active learning
4. Gives prompt feedback
5. Emphasizes time on task
6. Communicates high expectations
7. Respects diverse talents and ways of learning

Chickering and Gamson (1987) suggested that the actualization of these principles depends largely on the manipulation of campus environments. Accordingly, educators and administrators have the power to shape environments that promote "a strong sense of shared purposes; concrete support from administrators and faculty leaders for those purposes; adequate funding appropriate for the purposes; policies and procedures consistent with the purposes; and continuing examination of how well the purposes are being achieved" (p. 6). Furthermore, the authors maintained that the seven principles, when taken together, employ six powerful forces in education: activity, expectations, cooperation, interaction, diversity, and responsibility. These seven principles continue to serve as guidelines for determining institutional effectiveness in undergraduate education (Chickering and Gamson, 1999; Kuh and others, 2005) and have influenced the creation of good practice principles in other areas, such as student affairs.

The document *Principles of Good Practice for Student Affairs* served as a second model for this chapter. In 1996, leaders of the American College Personnel Association (ACPA) and the National Association of Student Personnel Administrators (NASPA) convened a study group of student affairs practitioners and faculty to construct a set of principles by which effectiveness in student affairs practice could be determined (ACPA and NASPA, 1997). According to Blimling and Whitt (1999), "The principles of good practice for student affairs are intended to build consensus on the actions associated with creating high-quality undergraduate experiences, thereby reinforcing a common agenda for student affairs—fostering student learning. . . . The principles are designed to be incorporated into our daily work and to shape how we think about our responsibilities, communicate our purposes, and interact with students" (pp. 203–204). To this end, good practice in student affairs:

1. Engages students in active learning
2. Helps students develop coherent values and ethical standards
3. Sets and communicates high expectations for student learning
4. Uses systematic inquiry to improve student and institutional performance
5. Uses resources effectively to achieve institutional missions and goals
6. Forges educational partnerships that advance student learning
7. Builds supportive and inclusive communities

In this chapter, we maintain that graduate and professional students would benefit from a corresponding set of principles to create quality experiences for, and enhance outcomes with, the population. The continued absence of such standards sustains a long-standing disconnect between these students, their academic programs and departments, and campuswide student affairs divisions. Taken together, student engagement is the primary emphasis of the principles offered by Chickering and Gamson (1987) and the ACPA/NASPA Study Group (1997). When we actualize the principles and engage students in learning, powerful gains and outcomes accrue (Kuh and others, 2005).

Gains and Outcomes Associated with Engagement

Based almost exclusively on undergraduate students, researchers have found that purposeful engagement, both inside and outside the classroom, positively affects a wide array of gains and outcomes that includes, but is not limited to, the following:

- Cognitive and intellectual skill development (Anaya, 1996; Baxter Magolda, 1992; Kuh, 1995; Ory and Braskamp, 1988; Pike, 2000)
- College adjustment (Cabrera and others, 1999; Delvin, 1996; Kuh, Palmer, and Kish, 2003; Paul and Kelleher, 1995)

- Moral and ethical development (Evans, 1987; Jones and Watt, 1999; Liddell and Davis, 1996; Rest, 1993)
- Persistence (Berger and Milem, 1999; Braxton, Milem, and Sullivan, 2000; Milem and Berger, 1997; Peltier, Laden, and Matranga, 1999; Tinto, 1993)
- Practical competence and skill transferability (Harper, 2005; Kuh, 1995; Kuh, Palmer, and Kish, 2003)
- Psychosocial development and positive images of self (Bandura, Peluso, Ortman, and Millard, 2000; Chickering and Reisser, 1993; Evans, Forney, and Guido-DiBrito, 1998; Taylor and Howard-Hamilton, 1995)

While it can be assumed that similar outcomes may be associated with active engagement for graduate and professional students, a set of guidelines for assessing the effects of such engagement is both lacking and necessary.

Seven Principles for Good Practice in Graduate Student Engagement

In this section, we offer a set of philosophical principles to guide student affairs efforts to foster graduate and professional student engagement and learning. We intend these principles to serve as a set of standards by which excellence in graduate education could be benchmarked and assessed. Using Chickering and Gamson (1987), the ACPA/NASPA Study Group (1997), and the large body of evidence related to the positive effects of student engagement, we crafted the seven principles presented below in response to the issues articulated by authors of other chapters in this volume. Regarding the engagement of graduate and professional students, we maintain that a student affairs division is most effective when it addresses these efforts:

1. *Continually strives to eradicate marginalization among underrepresented populations.* Good practice in graduate student engagement occurs when student affairs divisions offer support groups, special-interest student organizations, and mentoring programs for students in departments that lack racial/ethnic and gender diversity, as well as those in academic disciplines that typically enroll few students. The provision of such resources creates safe spaces in which the loneliness, cultural taxation, and feelings of discrimination that often characterize these students' experiences can be shared and processed (Patton and Harper, 2003). Efforts should be made to identify agents, both on campus and externally, who can offer culturally responsive support and advising to these students, especially those from smaller, racially homogeneous, and overwhelmingly male academic programs.

2. *Provides meaningful orientation to the institution beyond academic units.* Offering a coordinated and multiple-day series of orientation activities for new students and programs for prospective students that present the realities of graduate education constitutes good practice in graduate student

engagement. The importance of orientation for first-year undergraduate students is well understood: those who participate adjust more smoothly to the institution, are more familiar with campus resources, build more friendships earlier, and are more likely to persist than those who do not participate (Tinto, 1993). An effective student affairs division recognizes these same gains and outcomes as important for graduate and professional students. Although many academic schools and departments offer their own graduate orientations (typically a half-day or full day), they tend to emphasize only the norms, expectations, regulations, and resources within that respective unit (Boyle and Boice, 1998; Golde, 2000; Poock, 2002; Tierney and Rhoads, 1993). Furthermore, opportunities to form early relationships with others outside one's academic home are few. A well-conceived university-wide orientation introduces graduate and professional students to resources beyond their academic programs and departments, including campus offices, student organizations, and support outlets for underrepresented students; relies on advanced students to provide input on the content and format during the planning process, as well as leadership and mentorship during the actual orientation; and ultimately increases graduate student understanding of, and enthusiasm for, the institution.

3. *Invests resources in communication with graduate and professional students.* Good practice in graduate student engagement hinges on the timely distribution of important materials, announcements, and information to students. Exemplary student affairs divisions invest resources in the creation of brochures, newsletters, and Web sites for graduate and professional students. These divisions also partner with academic units to compile and disseminate information to graduate students about out-of-class engagement venues, leadership opportunities, campus resources, and upcoming events and deadlines, to name a few. Divisions ensure that graduate students are well represented as voting members on all relevant campus policy committees. Students perceive themselves to be knowledgeable about relevant aspects of the institution both within and outside their academic departments.

4. *Facilitates opportunities for community building and multicultural interaction across academic units.* Student learning is enhanced by planning, executing, and participating in purposeful campus activities, both educational and social (Kuh, 1995). Students learn best when they interact across difference (Chang, 1999; Gurin, Dey, Hurtado, and Gurin, 2002; Villalpando, 2002). Thus, good practice in graduate student engagement offers support and encouragement for students to build campuswide community through activities and organizations, especially those that emphasize cross-cultural interaction. The presence and availability of vibrant communities of difference confirm for students that they have networks of culturally diverse peers on whom they can rely for support, friendship, and value-added learning experiences beyond the classroom. Furthermore, as a side effect, the planning and execution of activities that lead to the advancement

New Directions for Student Services • DOI: 10.1002/ss

of community often produce the outcomes associated with active student engagement. Student affairs divisions partner with academic units to offer support, incentives, and resources (financial and otherwise) for graduate and professional students to create their own communities of engagement and support.

5. *Partners with academic schools and departments to create engagement plans for students.* Cooperation, meaningful dialogue, and strategic planning among student affairs professionals, faculty, student services staff within academic schools, academic affairs administrators, and students typify good practice. Engagement could, and should, be at the core of these conversations. Each stakeholder recognizes that the extent to which graduate and professional students are engaged in educationally purposeful experiences should not occur by happenstance. Thus, they collaboratively develop plans and strategies for connecting students to the larger campus community and positively affecting learning and outcomes beyond the classroom.

6. *Enhances career and professional development.* Good practice in career and professional development engages graduate and professional students in preparation for future roles. Effective career development centers expand their foci to include more outreach, workshops, services, counseling, and career fairs for graduate and professional students. Exemplary student affairs divisions, in cooperation with academic units and the graduate school, offer financial support for conference travel, especially for students who are presenting papers, workshops, or symposia. Institutional effectiveness can be easily ascertained by the credentials of its graduates. Those with impressive résumés and curriculum vitae that enable them to compete successfully for the most desirable opportunities after graduation are often beneficiaries of institutional investments.

7. *Systematically assesses satisfaction, needs, and outcomes.* Good practice in graduate student engagement involves ongoing data collection and analysis. Individual interviews and focus groups, as well as questionnaires and surveys, aid student affairs professionals in determining the affective dispositions of current and former graduate students toward campuswide programs and services. Assessments of how students change, what they learn outside the classroom, and the various ways in which they apply what they have learned through enriching educational experiences are deemed important and worthy of investigation. Data are shared within the division and with faculty, staff, and administrators in the various academic schools on campus. Findings shape future programming and interventions.

Conclusion

The purpose of the principles outlined above is to challenge and guide practitioners in expanding the role of student affairs to engage graduate students in educationally purposeful activities both inside and outside the classroom. This new role means that divisions of student affairs must expand their focus beyond undergraduates and incorporate the needs of graduate students.

Reexamining how student affairs engages graduate students means that existing services need to be modified and new programs created. By serving this new population, student affairs opens itself up to a wealth of opportunities for collaboration with academic affairs and graduate departments. While departments can do more to support their students, student affairs is positioned to engage graduate students across departments, provide improved campus services, and foster a campuswide graduate community.

References

American College Personnel Association and National Association of Student Personnel Administrators. *Principles of Good Practice for Student Affairs.* Washington, D.C.: American College Personnel Association and National Association of Student Personnel Administrators, 1997.

Anaya, G. "College Experiences and Student Learning: The Influence of Active Learning, College Environments, and Co-Curricular Activities." *Journal of College Student Development,* 1996, 37(6), 611–622.

Anderson, M. S., and Swazey, J. P. "Reflections on the Graduate Student Experience: An Overview." In M. S. Anderson (ed.), *The Experience of Being in Graduate School: An Exploration.* New Directions for Higher Education, no. 101. San Francisco: Jossey-Bass, 1998.

Astin, A. W. *What Matters in College? Four Critical Years Revisited.* San Francisco: Jossey-Bass, 1993.

Bair, C. R., and Haworth, J. G. "Doctoral Student Attrition and Persistence: A Meta-Synthesis of Research." Paper presented at the annual meeting of the Association for the Study of Higher Education, San Antonio, Tex., Nov. 1999.

Bandura, A., Peluso, E. A., Ortman, N., and Millard, M. "Effects of Peer Education Training on Peer Educators: Leadership, Self-Esteem, Health Knowledge, and Health Behaviors." *Journal of College Student Development,* 2000, 41(5), 471–478.

Baxter Magolda, M. B. "Cocurricular Influences on College Students' Intellectual Development." *Journal of College Student Development,* 1992, 33, 203–213.

Berger, J. B., and Milem, J. F. "The Role of Student Involvement and Perceptions of Integration in a Causal Model of Student Persistence." *Research in Higher Education,* 1999, 40(6), 641–664.

Blimling, G. S., and Whitt, E. J. (eds.). *Good Practice in Student Affairs: Principles to Foster Student Learning.* San Francisco: Jossey-Bass, 1999.

Bowen, W. G., and Rudenstine, N. L. *In Pursuit of the PhD.* Princeton, N.J.: Princeton University Press, 1992.

Boyle, P., and Boice, B. "Best Practices for Enculturation: Collegiality, Mentoring, and Structure." In M. S. Anderson (ed.), *The Experience of Being in Graduate School: An Exploration.* New Directions for Higher Education, no. 101. San Francisco: Jossey-Bass, 1998.

Braxton, J. M., Milem, J. F., and Sullivan, A. S. "The Influence of Active Learning on the College Departure Process: Toward a Revision of Tinto's Theory." *Journal of Higher Education,* 2000, 71(5), 569–590.

Cabrera, A. F., and others. "Campus Racial Climate and the Adjustment of Students to College: A Comparison Between White Students and African American Students." *Journal of Higher Education,* 1999, 70(2), 134–202.

Chang, M. J. "Does Racial Diversity Matter? The Educational Impact of a Racially Diverse Undergraduate Population." *Journal of College Student Development*, 1999, *40*(4), 377–395.

Chickering, A. W., and Gamson, Z. "Seven Principles for Good Practice in Undergraduate Education." *AAHE Bulletin*, 1987, *39*(7), 3–7.

Chickering, A. W., and Gamson, Z. "Development and Adaptations of the Seven Principles for Good Practice in Undergraduate Education." In M. D. Svinicki (ed.), *Teaching and Learning on the Edge of the Millennium: Building on What We Have Learned*. New Directions for Teaching and Learning, no. 80. San Francisco: Jossey-Bass, 1999.

Chickering, A. W., and Reisser, L. *Education and Identity*. (2nd ed.) San Francisco: Jossey-Bass, 1993.

Council of Graduate Schools. *Ph.D. Completion and Attrition: Policy, Numbers, Leadership, and Next Steps*. Washington, D.C.: Council of Graduate Schools, 2004.

Delvin, A. S. "Survival Skills Training During Freshman Orientation: Its Role in College Adjustment." *Journal of College Student Development*, 1996, *37*(3), 324–334.

Etzowitz, H., Kemelgor, C., Neuschatz, M., and Uzzi, B. "Athena Unbound: Barriers to Women in Academic Science and Engineering." *Science and Public Policy*, 1992, *19*(3), 157–179.

Evans, N. J. "A Framework for Assisting Student Affairs Staff in Fostering Moral Development." *Journal of Counseling and Development*, 1987, *66*, 191–193.

Evans, N. J., Forney, D. E., and Guido-DiBrito, F. *Student Development in College: Theory, Research, and Practice*. San Francisco: Jossey-Bass, 1998.

Fischer, B. A., and Zigmond, M. J. "Survival Skills for Graduate School and Beyond." In M. S. Anderson (ed.), *The Experience of Being in Graduate School: An Exploration*. New Directions for Higher Education, no. 101. San Francisco: Jossey-Bass, 1998.

Golde, C. M. "Beginning Graduate School: Explaining First-Year Doctoral Attrition." In M. S. Anderson (ed.), *The Experience of Being in Graduate School: An Exploration*. New Directions for Higher Education, no. 101. San Francisco: Jossey-Bass, 1998.

Golde, C. M. "Should I Stay or Should I Go? Student Descriptions of the Doctoral Attrition Process." *Review of Higher Education*, 2000, *23*(2), 199–227.

Gurin, P., Dey, E. L., Hurtado, S., and Gurin, G. "Diversity and Higher Education: Theory and Impact on Educational Outcomes." *Harvard Educational Review*, 2002, *72*(3), 330–366.

Harper, S. R. "Leading the Way: Inside the Experiences of High-Achieving African American Male Students." *About Campus*, 2005, *10*(1), 8–15.

Hartnett, R. T., and Katz, J. "The Education of Graduate Students." *Journal of Higher Education*, 1977, *48*(6), 646–664.

Jones, C. E., and Watt, J. D. "Psychosocial Development and Moral Orientation Among Traditional-Aged College Students." *Journal of College Student Development*, 1999, *40*, 125–132.

Jorgenson-Earp, C. R., and Staton, A. Q. "Student Metaphors for the College Freshman Experience." *Communication Education*, 1993, *42*, 123–141.

Kuh, G. D. "The Other Curriculum: Out-of-Class Experiences Associated with Student Learning and Personal Development." *Journal of Higher Education*, 1995, *66*(2), 123–155.

Kuh, G. D. "Setting the Bar High to Promote Student Learning." In G. S. Blimling and E. J. Whitt (eds.), *Good Practice in Student Affairs: Principles to Foster Student Learning*. San Francisco: Jossey-Bass, 1997.

Kuh, G. D. "Assessing What Really Matters to Student Learning: Inside the National Survey of Student Engagement." *Change*, 2001, *33*(3), 10–17.

Kuh, G. D., Palmer, M., and Kish, K. "The Value of Educationally Purposeful Out-of-Class Experiences." In T. L. Skipper and R. Argo (eds.), *Involvement in Campus Activities and the Retention of First-Year College Students*. Columbia: University of South Carolina, National Resource Center for the First-Year Experience and Students in Transition, 2003.

Kuh, G. D., and others. *Student Success in College: Creating Conditions That Matter.* San Francisco: Jossey-Bass, 2005.

Liddell, D. L., and Davis, T. L. "The Measure of Moral Orientation: Reliability and Validity Evidence." *Journal of College Student Development,* 1996, *37*(5), 485–493.

Lovitts, B. E. *Leaving the Ivory Tower: The Causes and Consequences of Departure from Doctoral Study.* Lanford, Md.: Rowan & Littlefield, 2001.

Milem, J. F., and Berger, J. B. "A Modified Model of College Student Persistence: Exploring the Relationship Between Astin's Theory of Involvement and Tinto's Theory of Student Departure." *Journal of College Student Development,* 1997, *38*(4), 387–400.

National Research Council. *Path to the Ph.D.: Measuring Graduate Attrition in the Sciences and Humanities.* Washington, D.C.: National Academy Press, 1996.

National Survey of Student Engagement. *Student Engagement, Pathways to Success: 2004 Annual Survey Results.* Bloomington, Ind.: Center for Postsecondary Research, National Survey of Student Engagement, 2004.

Nerad, M., and Miller, D. S. "Increasing Student Retention in Graduate and Professional Programs." In J. G. Haworth (ed.), *Assessing Graduate and Professional Education: Current Realities, Future Prospects.* New Directions for Institutional Research, no. 96. San Francisco: Jossey-Bass, 1996.

Ory, J., and Braskamp, L. "Involvement and Growth of Students in Three Academic Programs." *Research in Higher Education,* 1988, *28,* 116–129.

Pascarella, E. T. "Identifying Excellence in Undergraduate Education: Are We Even Close?" *Change,* 2001, *33*(3), 19–23.

Patton, L. D., and Harper, S. R. "Mentoring Relationships Among African American Women in Graduate and Professional Schools." In M. F. Howard-Hamilton (ed.), *Meeting the Needs of African American Women.* New Directions for Student Services, no. 104. San Francisco: Jossey-Bass, 2003.

Paul, E. L., and Kelleher, M. "Precollege Concerns About Losing and Making Friends in College: Implications for Friendship, Satisfaction and Self-Esteem During the College Transition." *Journal of College Student Development,* 1995, *36*(6), 513–521.

Peltier, G. L., Laden, R., and Matranga, M. "Student Persistence in College: A Review of Research." *Journal of College Student Retention,* 1999, *1*(4), 357–375.

Pike, G. R. "The Influence of Fraternity or Sorority Membership on Students' College Experiences and Cognitive Development." *Research in Higher Education,* 2000, *41,* 117–139.

Poock, M. C. "Graduate Student Orientation: Assessing Needs and Methods of Delivery." *Journal of College Student Development,* 2002, *43*(2), 231–245.

Pruitt-Logan, A. S., and Isaac, P. D. (eds.). *Student Services for a Changing Graduate Student Population.* New Directions for Student Services, no. 72. San Francisco: Jossey-Bass, 1995.

Rest, J. R. "Research on Moral Judgment in College Students." In A. Garrod (ed.), *Approaches to Moral Development.* New York: Teachers College Press, 1993.

Smallwood, S. "Doctor Dropout: High Attrition from Ph.D. Programs Is Sucking Away Time, Talent, and Money and Breaking Some Hearts, Too." *Chronicle of Higher Education,* Jan. 16, 2004, p. A10.

Taylor, C. M., and Howard-Hamilton, M. F. "Student Involvement and Racial Identity Attitudes Among African American Males." *Journal of College Student Development,* 1995, *36*(4), 330–336.

Tierney, W. G., and Rhoads, R. A. *Faculty Socialization as Cultural Process: A Mirror of Institutional Commitment.* ASHE-ERIC Higher Education Report, no. 6. Washington D.C.: George Washington School of Education and Development, 1993.

Tinto, V. *Leaving College: Rethinking the Causes and Cures of Student Attrition.* (2nd ed.) Chicago: University of Chicago Press, 1993.

U.S. Department of Education, National Center for Education Statistics. *Digest of Education Statistics, 2003.* Washington, D.C.: U.S. Department of Education, 2004.

U.S. Department of Education, National Center for Education Statistics. *Integrated Post-secondary Education Data System, Fall 2004.* Washington, D.C.: U.S. Department of Education, 2005.

Villalpando, O. "The Impact of Diversity and Multiculturalism on All Students: Findings from a National Study." *NASPA Journal,* 2002, *40*(1), 124–144.

JASON L. PONTIUS is the coordinator of graduate student life at the University of Maryland, College Park.

SHAUN R. HARPER is an assistant professor and research associate in the Center for the Study of Higher Education at the Pennsylvania State University.

NEW DIRECTIONS FOR STUDENT SERVICES • DOI: 10.1002/ss

5

This chapter discusses responsibilities for student affairs professionals in law and medical schools. It poses that student affairs staff are particularly suited to teach the hidden curriculum of the professional schools, described as inculcating professional values. The chapter ends with four strategies for such instruction.

The Hidden Curriculum in Medical and Law Schools: A Role for Student Affairs Professionals

Linda A. McGuire, Julie Phye

The education and development of students at the professional school level, in this case medical and law school, differs significantly from undergraduate and graduate school (Astin, 1993; Shulman, 2005). Students gain knowledge through large lectures and attend only a few small classes and seminars. Learning is split into didactic sessions and apprentice-type simulations of the profession. Large class size, with a much larger student-faculty ratio than graduate programs, increases the potential for student alienation, on the one hand, and for greater socialization by student peers rather than faculty mentors, on the other (Baird, 1995). In contrast to both undergraduate and graduate school, the enormous cost of professional education and the lack of in-school employment opportunities translate into a greater reliance on financial aid, for most students in the form of loans rather than grants. While academic support might be available and visible (Wangerin, 1988), most law and medical schools do not have designated support services for emotional or psychological issues, even though these may be more acute for law and medical students (Iijima, 1998; Dickerson, 1987).

Compared with their roles in undergraduate education, student affairs professionals in professional schools serve a similar and, at the same time, a unique role. Most medical and law schools have a person dedicated to student affairs work, but she or he might not have training or an educational background in student affairs. An informal review of student affairs officers

NEW DIRECTIONS FOR STUDENT SERVICES, no. 115, Fall 2006 © Wiley Periodicals, Inc.
Published online in Wiley InterScience (www.interscience.wiley.com) • DOI: 10.1002/ss.216

at top law schools indicated that a juris doctor degree seems to be required for student affairs officers, while only about half had any formal training beyond that degree, whether student affairs or not (Association of American Law Schools, 2004). Professional associations exist in medicine to provide staff development to those in student affairs roles. Depending on the size or philosophy of the school, the student affairs professional might serve roles filled by several people at the undergraduate level. In the course of a week, he or she might serve as academic advisor, registrar, and activities coordinator as well as offer advice on career planning and financial aid.

In this chapter, we explore the opportunities for student affairs staff to provide students with challenge and support (Sanford, 1962) in the unique environment of professional schools. After a description of the ways in which even routine student affairs tasks might differ in the medical and law school setting, we turn to a discussion of the ethical development of professional students. We then explore the concept of professionalism and why it has become a national concern in medical and legal preparation and practice. This chapter ends by describing tested strategies for student affairs staff to develop professional values among law and medical students. We conclude by encouraging student affairs professionals to consider how their work can have a positive impact on the development of professional school students.

Student Affairs in Professional Schools

Student affairs staff play an important role in professional school, though there are significant differences from undergraduate and graduate student affairs work. Most student development theory focuses on the needs of traditional undergraduates or older commuter students. Overlooked are the needs of professional students, which are just as prevalent and compelling as those of undergraduates. Like their peers, professional students encounter many developmental tasks outside the formal curriculum that provide an opportunity for student affairs involvement (Barr and others, 1993). Student affairs staff play critical roles related to academic advising, career planning, financial advising, and personal counseling.

Academic Advising. The needs for academic advising are great as professional students experience being academically average rather than the star of the class. For example, most law schools enforce a mandatory grading curve. While graduate students usually earn A's and B's that mirror their undergraduate grades, a law school entering class with a B+ or A undergraduate average must be graded on the full range of A to D grades. Students accustomed to earning A's and B's in college might find themselves earning C's and D's in law school.

In addition, the amount of information and the pace at which students must ingest and assimilate new knowledge are considerably different from undergraduate classes (Iijima, 1998). Bright students are forced to abandon old methods of studying that no longer keep pace with the amount of material set out in the curriculum. Studying and test-taking strategies are highly sought skills often taught by a counselor or student affairs professional. In the undergraduate experience, tutor groups are often assumed to be designed for students who have below-average grades. In medicine, however, tutor groups are arranged by student affairs staff as a standard component of a successful course of study engaged in by any student. Student affairs professionals can assist professional students in adjusting to the academic demands of law or medical school and can provide necessary tools to foster student success.

Career Planning. One might assume that once they are accepted into professional school, students exhibit little need for further career advising. To the contrary, the legal and medical student's career exploration and advising is ongoing. Students must explore the many specializations within the practice of both law and medicine. They must begin from their first year of professional school to define their area of interest so as to take advantage of practical, job shadowing, or volunteer work that will distinguish them from other students. Student affairs staff provide consistent, ongoing advice and contacts for students as they progress through professional school and consider their career options.

Students in medicine are provided a peer mentor and faculty advisor during their first year. In medicine, the third year is primarily a survey of clerkships in the hospital to acquaint students with the different disciplines of medicine and surgery. Student affairs staff help medical students weigh professional interests, abilities, and personal needs against the many requirements of the various disciplines within medicine.

Law students' success in postgraduation employment might depend on their own industriousness, albeit with the guidance of career services staff. Unlike matches that link medical students with postgraduation residencies, law students direct their own job search, with summer jobs often blossoming into permanent offers. Law students benefit from professional help in identifying their interests as well as locating positions.

Financial Advising. Student affairs staff play an important role in financial advising. The cost of professional school is dramatically higher than a typical undergraduate or graduate education. Although the earning potential on completion is also greater, considerable debt is accrued in professional school from high tuition, multiple lab fees, instruments, and specialized examinations. This debt load directly affects the range of job choices for law students, as the salaries earned in public interest positions are often insufficient to make loan payments. Due to the intense academic demands, students are discouraged from working, so there is little opportunity to offset the expenses while in school. Aid packages and scholarships are often available, but the assistance of a college's financial officer is necessary to keep current with selection criteria for the different monies available. It is not unusual for a graduate in law or medicine from a public midwestern university to leave with $100,000 of loans to repay. Helping the student to navigate the criteria and deadlines of aid and scholarship packages is an important responsibility of student affairs professionals.

Personal Counseling. Student affairs professionals play an important role in listening, offering advice, and referring students to additional resources as they face a host of personal and professional issues. First, listening to and guiding students as they define their professional identity is a valuable charge of the student affairs staff. Medical students write in their personal statements about their interest in serving the community and their desire to ease others' suffering. Realizing that goal in the light of a demanding curriculum is a daunting task. Student affairs staff can anchor students and keep them focused on their reasons for entering medical or law school.

Second, professional and graduate students are more likely than undergraduates to commit to a partnered relationship or start a family. Other students are in the process of coming out as gay, lesbian, bisexual, or transgendered. Working toward a career in law or medicine is rewarding, but spending countless hours dedicated to learning one's profession can put stressors on familial relationships.

Third, professional students experience personal counseling needs as do other students, but they might be hesitant to pursue counseling resources. For instance, medical students who experience depression might have counseling resources available but choose not to use them (Tjia, Givens, and Shea, 2005). With regard to personal counseling needs, both intra- and interpersonal, establishing connections with incoming students, providing resource information for all students, and providing referrals as well as the encouragement to use such referrals constitute important work for student affairs professionals.

Finally, students in professional school experience unique challenges to their spiritual or philosophical identity. From their first semester, medical students are exposed to conversations on death and dying. By their second year, they participate in patient simulation sessions to practice delivering bad news. Similarly, despite their hard work on clients' behalf, law students in clinics watch clients go to prison or lose their children. Faculty members in these programs guide students analytically and perhaps emotionally. Student affairs staff also represent a valuable resource for students at this time to listen, ask questions, and validate the many feelings students have.

Values Inculcation in Professional School

Aside from the practical distinctions between graduate and professional education described in the previous section, medical and law curricula have been called "signature pedagogies" (Shulman, 2005) because of their similarity from school to school. The course of study mirrors the demands of professional life and develops intellectual excellence as well as enculturation into the medical and legal professions' distinct ethics and values.

NEW DIRECTIONS FOR STUDENT SERVICES • DOI: 10.1002/ss

Students come into law and medical schools expecting to be intellectually challenged, study long hours, and compete with their classmates for good grades. In large lecture classes, their expectations of intellectual challenge are met. A graduating lawyer or physician must be committed to a lifetime of learning new information and skills (American Bar Association, 1992). Legal and medical education consequently stress the requirement of self-teaching and acquiring the skills necessary to analyze new problems and keep up with a changing body of knowledge. This approach contrasts with the creation of new knowledge emphasized by graduate programs.

In addition, because lawyers and physicians take on the responsibility for their clients' or patients' health, lives, livelihoods, and liberty, entry into professional practice requires more than earning the terminal academic degree. Like other professionals, such as psychologists, physicians and lawyers must pass licensure exams and fitness and character inquiries. Even after licensure, they face lifelong regulation by governmental and professional entities and, in many areas, a requirement of annual continuing education.

Adding to this demand of professional competence to practice an area of law or medicine and the commitment to lifelong learning, law and medical students must see themselves as part of a profession. This profession not only claims a distinct body of learning and skills but embraces a core set of values that sets them apart from the rest of society, joining them together as brethren. As a professional, a lawyer or doctor is expected to be a contributor to the community, a role model of service (Cohen, 2002).

The term *professionalism* has been used to describe the adherence to a set of values beyond intellectual capacity that is common to the professions and gives practitioners the exclusive right to engage in the profession's activities (American Bar Association, 1992). For purposes of this discussion, there are two types of professionalism. The first regards how the student conducts himself or herself with respect to the educational program. The second follows the preparation, both formal and informal, of students to deal with the responsibility and trust bestowed on them by clients or patients. The values incorporated in both definitions of professionalism include altruism, accountability, honor and integrity, sense of duty, and respect for others (Robins, Braddock, and Fryer-Edwards, 2002).

- Altruism. During their training, law and medical students find themselves in transition from the role of student, who is at the center of education, to the altruistic practitioner, who focuses on the best interest of the client or patient. The tension might be heightened in law school where competition for top grades can be fierce and students' contact with clients may be minimal. This task proves difficult in medicine as well, as students repeatedly strive to balance their own learning with the care of their patients.
- Accountability. Professional students are accountable for behavioral infractions to their college dean, whereas undergraduates typically are held accountable by a dean of students rather than an academic department.

Papadakis, Osborn, Cooke, and Healy (1999) illustrated that problematic behavior in medical school was associated with subsequent disciplinary action by a state medical board. In professional school, then, students' behavior is subject to discipline not only by the schools but by the professions as well. Students must understand that these professions are accountable to society to address the needs of the public. State and national licensure and certifications build that accountability further.

• Honor and integrity. "Honor and integrity" entails the constant regard for high standards of behavior and communication. Students of law and medicine must be aware that they must meet higher standards of behavior than most graduate or undergraduate students. Students are challenged to recognize they are entering professions in which past failures to meet these standards have changed the public perception of lawyers and doctors.

• Sense of duty. Duty is synonymous with commitment to service. Physicians and lawyers must be readily available and compassionate when their patients or clients need them. As they begin their education, professional students forfeit personal time and freedom in order to meet the demands of their professions. The demands of their education and, later, of their careers, often impinge on the expectations of their families. The advent of the eighty-hour workweek is an effort by the medical profession to assist resident physicians in combining duty and family.

• Respect for others. Paramount to professionalism is respect for others. To be a respected lawyer or physician, one must respect one's patients or clients and their families. It is no less important to show respect for one's instructors and colleagues. Respect for peers enhances collegiality among physicians and lawyers, contributing to better care or representation of patients and clients.

Given the lifelong expectations of practicing lawyers and physicians, one might think that considerable attention would be paid by legal and medical educators to developing their students' professional values. Unlike undergraduate schools, especially public universities, that have abandoned moral or values education in part to avoid the risk of impinging on particular cultural or religious beliefs (Evans, 1987; Modjeska, 1991), law and medical schools have an explicit or implicit mandate to do so. Furthermore, in contrast to traditional-aged college students, the vast majority of law and medical students are in their mid- to late twenties, an ideal time for development of professional values and moral reasoning (Guthrie, 1977).

In contrast to the academy's adeptness in honing intellectual prowess, however, the development of other professional skills and values might be less the focus of students and instructors alike (Arnold, 2002). Although professional schools require students to take a course in professional responsibility or ethics, the focus of the class is on understanding the substance of the requirements rather than on integrating professional expectations into one's daily life (Wegner, 2004).

NEW DIRECTIONS FOR STUDENT SERVICES • DOI: 10.1002/ss

This is not to suggest that students have no opportunity to develop professional values through the standard curriculum. Leadership positions in student-run, credit-granting co-curricular programs, such as serving as an editor in charge of other students who are writing for a law journal, provide possibilities for developing leadership, compassion, responsibility, and the like. Clinical settings in both legal and medical education similarly permit students to try on the role of a fully functioning professional. Students' participation in these clinics might be accompanied by a suitable marker of having entered the profession, such as the white coat ceremony (described below) for medical students or, for law students, being provisionally admitted to law practice and sworn in by a judge.

We believe that the development of professional values constitutes the hidden curriculum of professional schools (Arnold, 2002). It is often undertaken outside the classroom and is therefore a suitable topic for consideration by student affairs staff in professional schools.

Student Affairs Strategies to Help Medical and Law Students Make the Transition from Student to Professional

We describe four programs, two in each of our environments, that are commonplace in medical and law schools. We do not suggest them as programmatic innovations as much as illustrations of how one might focus on professional values development in the ordinary work of student affairs professionals.

Medical School Ceremonies. Several ceremonies mark students' progression through medical school and into the medical profession. Teaching professional values in medicine begins at the end of orientation with the white coat ceremony. Three days of orientation conclude with a ceremony marking the new students' acceptance into the medical culture. Over the course of orientation, student affairs professionals help new medical students with their white coat fittings. During this process, student affair professionals talk to the new matriculates about their goals as they enter medical school.

The white coat ceremony demonstrates for students the transition from student into a profession guided by the values of duty, integrity, and respect for others. Students and their families gather in an auditorium to receive a formal address on the magnificent honor and responsibility that is inherent in the role of the physician. The presenting physician discusses the high standards and accountability that will be bestowed on the students as they begin their journey to becoming physicians. New students don their first white coat and recite the Hippocratic oath for the first time. This ceremony marks the transition from student to student-physician and alerts students to their professional responsibility for others' health and well-being.

After two years of classroom learning, students are ready to shift their education to the clinical arena. The Gold Humanism student clinician ceremony marks the transition to beginning clinical learning in the hospital and the students' role to one of student-clinician. The Gold Humanism Society provides a week of intensive training of clinical skills that culminates in a luncheon with an address from a physician deemed by the students to represent humanism in medicine. Students each receive a book relevant to the art of medicine and are encouraged to remember the ideals with which they came to medical school. The student-clinician ceremony strives to remind each student that he or she will now learn not from textbooks but from observing and interacting with actual patients. Accountability, altruism, and respect for others are values that students will develop as their learning environment shifts from the classroom to hospital wards.

Although student affairs professionals have little involvement in the actual ceremony, their influence is felt in the time leading up to the ceremony. They work daily with the students as they hone their skills at taking patient histories, conducting physical exams, and creating case management plans. Students talk informally with student affairs staff about the type of physician they hope to become, how they hope to focus on the needs of their patients, and what kind of colleague they hope to be. These conversations represent important opportunities for student affairs professionals to introduce and reinforce the values of the medical profession. Indeed, it is critical for student affairs professionals to be mindful of, and incorporate into their practice, not only the mission of the school but of the profession as well. Doing so allows staff to help students develop an understanding and conviction of the professional values inherent in the culture of medicine.

Law School Application Procedure. Unlike the medical school white coat ceremony, law schools do not have traditions or discrete events to signify to students that they are entering a service profession. Orientation programs, which are common in law schools, do provide an opportunity, however, for new students to begin to internalize important professional values—for example, self-governance, integrity, and forthrightness (McGuire, 2004).

At the Iowa Law School, a mandatory session for new students, "The Legal Profession: Conduct and Fitness Expectations," introduces to them the bar's character and fitness investigations and connects the law student conduct codes to the bar's similar rules. A member of the Iowa Board of Law Examiners explains the process for students interested in practicing in Iowa to register that intent, so that an early background investigation can flag reasons that would block admission to the bar three years later. Students are informed that they must disclose all law infractions, including traffic violations and juvenile offenses. They are also warned that failure to disclose background information is usually more serious than the record of the substantive offenses itself.

As a result of this program, we have learned that significant numbers of students have hidden past misconduct on their law school applications. Up to 10 percent of the incoming class at Iowa in the past few years admitted to these omissions (McGuire, 2004). These cases would have been appropriate for action under the law school's misconduct code, but student affairs personnel believed that treating these cases as misconduct would miss an important opportunity for professional development, if only in beginning stages. Merely punishing application misrepresentation cases would approach the student conduct at the lowest levels of ethical decision making: an appeal to right behavior to avoid negative consequences. Rather, in the orientation session, new law students are invited to review their law school applications and initiate amendment requests if they failed to disclose criminal or other misconduct history.

This application amendment and amnesty procedure focuses on two important aspects of professionalism that arise in that context: correcting a common misconception about the nature of lawyers' work and introducing the concept of the role-differentiated behavior of lawyers. Situating the application amendment process in the context of a law school orientation program that welcomes them to a new profession permits a subtle shift from an appeal to right behavior solely to avoid negative consequences to one that appeals to students to act out of a sense of professional obligation.

First, the application amendment process seeks to make the point that the legal profession values honesty and self-disclosure over self-promotion. The amendment process attempts to counteract a common misconception about lawyer behavior among new students, and perhaps among the public at large: that it is the role of lawyers to engage in fact spinning and stretching, a type of zealous advocacy that students called "lawyering." Applicants had failed to disclose all relevant background information, some claimed, because they were "lawyering" their way through the application questions. This type of advocacy is arguably appropriate when representing a criminal client but is almost always inappropriate when reporting information about oneself.

The second shift goes beyond transmitting information about legal professional values. An application amendment process can be an interactive learning process that provides an opportunity to engage in a form of critical reasoning that is a mark of moral development (Richards, 1981). One of the ethical requirements of lawyers' work is to exercise independent professional judgment (American Bar Association, 1992). By engaging in conversation with students who ask to amend their applications we encourage them to shift from relying on others' advice ("My dad/the judge/police officer said I'd never have to disclose this juvenile offense") to developing their own judgment ("Why won't you tell me whether I am required by the application question to disclose this prior offense? I have to make that decision myself?"). The potential for developing critical thinking and moral analysis, though perhaps haphazard and modest, can be exploited in the application amendment process. It is the law school student affairs professional (the dean of students or admissions officer) who is positioned to guide students through these processes.

Integrated Medical Learning Communities. Learning communities in medicine are based in student development theory and provide medical students a way to create connections and decrease the isolation they often feel. Learning communities are the vehicle through which student affairs staff, called community coordinators, design, implement, and evaluate activities and programs that develop medical students' social, emotional, and ethical development as well as leadership skills. Learning communities in medicine are an intentional model for breaking down class barriers, increasing peer leadership, increasing formal faculty contact, and promoting professional values.

At the University of Iowa's Carver College of Medicine, four nonresidential learning communities are named in honor of faculty who exemplified professional values during their career. Vertical integration across the matriculated classes yields a community of 140 students, with a quarter of the members coming from each class. Each community is supported architecturally through dedicated space provided in the college and the presence of dedicated staff members. Each community has a full-time coordinator who has experience in student affairs. In addition, a .25 full-time-equivalent faculty director who is a practicing physician is part of the team that implements the learning community philosophy and model.

The tenets on which communities were founded include support for student success through centrally managed counseling and mentoring. Vertical integration encourages students to relate to upper-class students, faculty, and staff and to model humanistic behavior and appreciation for diversity. Teaching the professional values of duty, altruism, and respect for others occurs through leadership development and community service. Developing student leadership is achieved by skills training and skill application to community government structure. Community service and self-directed learning are critical goals that are important to the success of the communities. Communities have gained the respect of the students, staff, and faculty as a means for coming together for mentoring, career counseling, ethical concerns, and appreciative inquiry. As community coordinators, student affairs professionals help guide the development of communities as learning environments where students learn, develop, and integrate professional values into their professional identities.

Service-Learning. Service-learning represents an additional tool used in law schools to teach professional values outside the classroom. Part of a national initiative, service-learning is defined as a teaching and learning strategy that integrates meaningful community service with instruction and reflection to build skills, teach civic responsibility, and build community (Treuthart, 2003; Smith, 2004). It differs from volunteering in the community in that it seeks to improve both the student and the community. While increasingly commonplace in K–12 and undergraduate education, the shift highlighted in professional schools entails the learning and reflection as an introduction to professional values.

A law school's service-learning experience, if it were to focus on professionalism, would add two aspects to pure volunteerism. The first occurs merely by setting the program in the long-articulated tradition in the legal profession that may require lawyers, as a condition of licensure, to contribute their time to serve persons of lesser means who cannot afford legal services (American Bar Association, 2004). While each state is free to modify, qualify, or limit this requirement as a practical matter, the tradition of pro bono publico ("for the good of the public") is a universally accepted aspiration or expectation of those admitted to legal practice. Situating service-learning in this context introduces students to the professional concept of pro bono work.

The second aspect of using service-learning to teach professionalism is less didactic, though equally cognitive and distinctly more personal. When law schools incorporate service-learning into the curriculum, they are no longer simply lecturing students about the long-held professional tradition of pro bono publico. In a service-learning program for law students, the learning also invites students to confront and internalize the underlying values in the traditional requirement of pro bono service. One such value is humility—understanding that membership in the legal profession puts one in an elite position in society. Lawyers have the power to affect justice by deciding whose interests to represent. Unfortunately, whether justice prevails is often determined by whether the citizen is a person of means and can afford the expensive services of an attorney.

The reflection component of service-learning for law students comes when they acknowledge the privilege they enjoy in both coming to law school and practicing law. This reflection is more powerful when they work alongside people of limited means. A clinical colleague describes the transformation he sees in the students whom he takes to hold Spanish-language, immigrant client intake clinics in a nearby working-class community. The students' transformation is deeply personal; they become better people, not just better lawyers, for having served this clientele.

Other legal educators have recognized that legal clinical education affords students this type of learning through reflection (Smith, 2004). Service-learning need not be limited to the clinic or other credit programs, however. It must nonetheless require reflection on personal growth and professional values to distinguish it from pure volunteer activity. Cleaning a highway might be a good community service activity conducted by a legal service fraternity, but it likely will not cause students to reflect deeply on the profession they are entering. True service-learning outside the classroom stands a better chance of focusing on professional values when student affairs staff, trained or experienced in student development theory, guide the process of self-reflection.

Conclusion

Many opportunities for student affairs work exist in professional schools. The needs of professional students are many and often differ from those of undergraduate and graduate students. Fenske (1989) reminds us that the mission of the college is to educate the whole student, not only his or her intellect. Student affairs professionals are uniquely situated not only to provide such traditional services as advising and career planning to professional students but also to influence student learning and growth through the development and inculcation of professional values. We consider this opportunity crucial for the development of professional students and encourage our colleagues in students affairs to consider the impact they could have on practice and scholarship in professional schools.

References

American Bar Association. *Model Rules of Professional Conduct.* Eagan, Minn.: West, 2004.

American Bar Association, Section of Legal Education and Admissions to the Bar, Legal Education and Professional Development. *Report of the Task Force on Law Schools and the Profession: Narrowing the Gap.* Chicago: American Bar Association, 1992.

Arnold, L. "Assessing Professional Behavior: Yesterday, Today and Tomorrow." *Academic Medicine,* 2002, 77(6), 502–515.

Astin, A. W. *What Matters in College: Four Critical Years Revisited.* San Francisco: Jossey-Bass, 1993.

Baird, L. "Helping Graduate Students: A Graduate Adviser's View." In A. S. Pruitt-Logan and P. D. Isaac (eds.), *Student Services for the Changing Graduate Student Population.* New Directions for Student Services, no. 72. San Francisco: Jossey-Bass, 1995.

Barr, M., and others (eds.). *Handbook of Student Affairs Administration.* San Francisco: Jossey-Bass, 1993.

Cohen, J. "Our Compact with Tomorrow's Doctors." *Academic Medicine,* 2002, 77(6), 475–480.

Dickerson, F. "Psychological Counseling for Law Students: One Law School's Experience." *Journal of Legal Education,* 1987, 37(1), 82–90.

Evans, N. "A Framework for Assisting Student Affairs Staff in Fostering Moral Development." *Journal of Counseling and Development,* 1987, 66(4), 191–194.

Fenske, R. "Evolution of the Student Services Professional." In U. Delworth and others (eds.), *Student Services: A Handbook for the Profession.* (2nd ed.) San Francisco: Jossey-Bass, 1989.

Guthrie, V. "Cognitive Foundations of Ethical Development." *New Directions for Student Services,* 1977, 23, 28–31.

Iijima, A. "Lessons Learned: Legal Education and Law Student Dysfunction." *Journal of Legal Education,* 1998, 48(4), 524–538.

McGuire, L. "Lawyering or Lying? When Law School Applicants Hide Their Criminal Histories and Other Misconduct." *South Texas Law Review,* 2004, 45(4), 709–751.

Modjeska, L. "On Teaching Morality to Law Students." *Journal of Legal Education,* 1991, 41(1), 71–74.

Papadakis, M., Osborn, E., Cooke, M., and Healy, K. "A Strategy for the Detection and Evaluation of Unprofessional Behavior in Medical Students." *Academic Medicine,* 1999, 74(8), 980–990.

Richards, D. "Moral Theory: The Developmental Psychology of Ethical Autonomy and Professionalism." *Journal of Legal Education,* 1981, 31(3), 359–374.

Robins, L., Braddock, C., and Fryer-Edwards, K. "Using the American Board of Internal Medicine's 'Elements of Professionalism' for Undergraduate Ethics Education." *Academic Medicine,* 2002, 77(6), 523–531.

Sanford, N. *The American College.* Hoboken, N.J.: Wiley, 1962.

Shulman, L. "The Signature Pedagogies of the Professions of Law, Medicine, Engineering, and the Clergy: Potential Lessons for the Education of Teachers." 2005. Retrieved Oct. 3, 2005, from http://hub.mspnet.org/media/data/Shulman_Signature_Pedagogies.pdf.

Smith, L. "Why Clinical Programs Should Embrace Civic Engagement, Service Learning, and Community Based Research." *Clinical Law Review*, 2004, *10*(2), 773–754.

Tjia, J., Givens, J., and Shea, J. "Factors Associated with Undertreatment of Medical Student Depression." *Journal of American College Health*, 2005, *53*(5), 219–224.

Treuthart, M. "Weaving a Tapestry—Providing Context Through Service Learning." *Gonzaga Law Review*, 2003, *38*(1), 215–236.

Wangerin, P. "Objective, Multiplistic, and Relative Truth in Developmental Psychology and Legal Education." *Tulane Law Review*, 1988, *62*, 1237–1301.

Wegner, J. "Better Writing, Better Thinking: Thinking Like a Lawyer." *Legal Writing: Journal of Legal Writing Instruction*, 2004, *10*, 9–21.

LINDA A. MCGUIRE *is associate dean of student affairs at the University of Iowa College of Law.*

JULIE PHYE *is associate director of curriculum at the University of Iowa, Carver College of Medicine.*

6

Career services tailored to the needs of graduate and professional students constitute an important strategy for fostering student success. Career services can help graduate and professional students explore careers outside academe, prepare for academic and nonacademic job searches, and make the transition from graduate school to professional positions.

Career Services for Graduate and Professional Students

Tom Lehker, Jennifer S. Furlong

> I just think we need to ask ourselves what we are asking of the employers. Are we asking them to hire us because we really want the job and think we can perform well? Are we asking them to hire us because we just think we deserve good jobs because of our degrees? Or are we asking them to hire us because we can't find the job we really want and we need something to tide us over until we can find a teaching job? You have to be realistic about your chances of getting a job if you hold the last two attitudes. No one owes us anything.
>
> Woodrow Wilson National Fellowship Foundation (2000)

These sentences, written by a graduate student on a career options listserv, raise a number of vital career development issues facing graduate and professional students. Evidence suggests that today's system of graduate education does not adequately prepare students for the needs of a changing workforce (Nyquist and Wulff, 2000). Significant proportions of doctoral students, for instance, will pursue careers outside the academy because of a lack of available positions in higher education (LaPidus, 1998). Career services can prove instrumental in fostering graduate students' career development. By providing comprehensive career services for graduate and professional students, campuses can help realize the goal of producing "scholar-citizens who see their special training connected more closely to the needs of society and the global economy" (Nyquist and Wulff, 2000, p. 2).

NEW DIRECTIONS FOR STUDENT SERVICES, no. 115, Fall 2006 © Wiley Periodicals, Inc.
Published online in Wiley InterScience (www.interscience.wiley.com) • DOI: 10.1002/ss.217

The Need for Career Services for Graduate Students

Generally, the experience of graduate and professional students in their respective programs has been described as one of socialization (Weidman, Twale, and Stein, 2001). The goal of graduate and professional programs is not only to impart academic material to students, but also to help them take on a new social role. Weidman and Stein (2003) write, "A central purpose of postbaccalaureate education, particularly at the doctoral level, is the socialization of individuals into the cognitive and affective dimensions of social roles related to the practice of learned occupations" (p. 642). On completion of their programs, graduate and professional students are assumed to have taken on a professional identity that is appropriate to their desired career outcomes. This socialization process, however, does not address necessarily the career needs of graduate and professional students.

As suggested in previous chapters, individuals enter graduate and professional education from a variety of backgrounds and with a variety of personal characteristics and experiences. They hold diverse interests and engage in diverse academic pursuits. Some enroll in professional master's degree programs in fields such as business, nursing, engineering, or education. Others pursue doctoral and master's degrees in traditional research areas. Because graduate and professional students have selected an academic field of study specialized beyond the bachelor's degree, they often are assumed to need no career guidance (Luzzo, 2000).

To the contrary, significant numbers of students enter graduate studies as a way to explore career options (Luzzo, 2000) and thus could benefit from services designed to help them identify and explore their career interests. Indeed, over the past decade, calls for career guidance for graduate students, particularly doctoral students, have become increasingly prevalent (see, for example, Golde and Dore, 2001; LaPidus, 1995, 1998; Luzzo, 2000). Doctoral students typically expect to find an academic position in their field of study (LaPidus, 1995; Golde and Dore, 2001). In a study of four thousand doctoral students in eleven disciplines at twenty-seven institutions, Golde and Dore (2001) found that most doctoral students were planning for a career in academe, though this varied by discipline, and most doctoral students reported being ill prepared for the role of faculty member. The authors also noted that most doctoral students would not find work as tenure-track faculty members. According to LaPidus (1995), the availability of academic positions has diminished as the numbers of Ph.D. holders has increased.

The realities of the job market, both academic and nonacademic, stand in contrast to student expectations (Golde and Dore, 2001; LaPidus, 1995, 1998). Although doctoral students expect to have academic careers (Golde and Dore, 2001), roughly 50 percent of Ph.D. recipients pursue nonacademic positions (LaPidus, 1998). This phenomenon takes place in the context of an education that does not entail preparation for specific jobs outside the academy (LaPidus, 1995). Furthermore, perceived mismatches between student expectations and realities of graduate work, and the implications of those realities for students' perceived career options, have been noted as contributing to student attrition (Nerad and Miller, 1996). To address these and other discrepancies, advocates for graduate education have called for improved job information and career guidance for graduate students (Golde and Dore, 2001; LaPidus, 1995, 1998; Luzzo, 2000; Nerad and Miller, 1996; Nyquist and Wulff, 2000). As a result, colleges and universities have begun to provide career services programs and information tailored to meet the specific needs of graduate and professional students.

Providing Career Services on Campus

The need and importance of providing career services to graduate students is clear. Less clear is the best or most effective way to provide those services. Which units consider themselves to be delivering career services to graduate and professional school students, and how can these units work collaboratively? How should services be developed to ensure that they are meeting the needs of graduate students? We begin with a brief discussion of the premises for providing graduate career services and follow with a discussion of approaches to providing such services.

Premises. Based on our experiences of working with graduate students, we offer two premises for providing career services. First, graduate students will be drawn to services and resources they believe are designed specifically for them. They understand that their needs are often different from those of undergraduates and might be wary of an office or a service that does not recognize their unique perspective. Regardless of how career services are provided, the campus must make efforts to develop and communicate services and resources that speak directly to the graduate student experience.

Second, there is no one-size-fits-all approach to career services for graduate students. What works at one institution might be impractical at another for a variety of reasons. The needs and resources of individual academic units on campus might dictate a range of models that work effectively. Several factors, including the resources of academic units and the strengths of a career services unit, determine the effectiveness for each situation.

Approaches to Providing Services. Given the lack of a one-size-fits-all model for graduate career services, a number of approaches exist for providing such services. Among them are centralized services, academically based career services, campus collaborations, and developmental approaches.

Centralized Services. A centralized career services office enables graduate students to use well-developed services already in place. On-campus recruiting, job fairs, self-assessment instruments, career counseling, and many other resources can be adapted to serve the needs of graduate students. A centralized office, often falling under the purview of student affairs, can be a convenient place for employers with diverse hiring needs to reach students from a wide range of academic backgrounds.

Centralized career services are often provided by staff with student and career development training and expertise (Kroll and Rentz, 1988). Although graduate students have unique concerns when compared with undergraduates, they also share many of the core student and career development issues (Stewart, 1995):

- What are my skills, interests, and values, and how do these affect my career decisions?
- What career options are available to me, and how do I begin to explore and make sense of them?
- How do I conduct a job search? What is involved in that process?

These issues are a part of the daily conversation in a student affairs–based career services office, and students will benefit from working with staff who take a developmental approach to their work. In addition, career services staff bring well-honed counseling skills, awareness of the world of work, and expertise on how to access career information from a wide range of sources, all of which can be helpful to the graduate and professional student population.

Finally, and not to be underestimated, the career services office can be perceived by graduate students as a safe or at least neutral place to access when exploring career options that fall outside the norm for an academic unit. Graduate students might feel pressure to conform to certain expectations related to career decision making and uncomfortable talking about alternatives with advisors or others in their department (Stewart, 1995).

A centralized approach is not without challenges. A career services office that has traditional-age undergraduates as its most frequent users might be perceived by students, staff, and faculty as being just for undergraduates. Graduate students may be skeptical whether a career services office is ready to work with them. Especially on larger and more comprehensive campuses, graduate students represent an extremely diverse group, from sixteen-month terminal master's students to doctoral students of every conceivable discipline. Career professionals cannot be expected to be experts on each discipline or to know each individual student very well.

A centralized office with an environment that feels more intentionally welcoming to graduate students can mitigate these challenges. Career service providers must start by understanding, as much as possible, the disciplinary and departmental issues important to career development for groups of students and for individuals. Programs and services designed specifically for graduate students, provided by staff with training specific to the needs of graduate students, can signal the campus that career services is interested and ready to address the needs of all students.

Academically Based Career Services. Career services provided by academic units, either within individual departments or through the graduate college, can provide many benefits not possible through a centralized approach. Departments bring expertise in the discipline, often a critical part of the career development process, and department staff tend to be more closely connected to individual students.

Career services offered through an academic unit come with an inherent academic stamp of approval, sending the message that career services matter and that students should take advantage of them. Graduate college staff are uniquely situated to develop close relationships with other units that might bear on career issues for students, such as a fellowships office or a center for teaching and learning.

Conversely, an academic unit providing career services might not derive the benefits of an economy of scale that often come with a centralized office. Career services through an academic department might consist of an office of one person—or just a part-time person in this role—without the ability to develop the types of robust services available to a larger and more developed office. Academically based staff might have limited knowledge of career options as well as the career development process.

Campus Collaborations. In all likelihood, a campus will not employ only one model of career services, either through a centralized office or academic units. Instead, career services might be accessed from a variety of sources. Collaboration and communication become the keys for this approach to be successful. Staff and faculty who provide career support must be aware of each other and offer services that reflect the strengths of each unit in a complementary way. Career services providers can also look for other natural collaborators on topics related to career and professional development for graduate students, such as counseling and psychological services. Smart collaborations can stretch campus resources and provide a more coherent package of career-related services for students.

A Developmental Approach. Regardless of how services are provided, graduate student career issues must be placed in the context of other developmental and life issues that students face. We know, anecdotally and from the literature, that graduate students bring many factors to career decision making that are not as common for undergraduates—in terms of age, life experiences, family and financial issues, and questions of identity, to name just a few (Golde and Dore, 2001). Career services providers must be aware of these issues and how they bear on students' career decisions.

As we increase our understanding of the developmental stages and challenges that graduate students experience, we must also develop services and resources that are grounded in that information. Stewart (1995), for example, offered a framework for understanding the graduate student experience as being organized around three developmental stages: entry, engagement, and exit. Each stage offers an explanation of some of the typical challenges students face during their academic careers. Developing a greater understanding of models of graduate student development, such as those discussed in Chapter Two in this volume, will help create resources that are responsive to the needs of this student population.

Working with Doctoral and Research Master's Students

Over the past several years, national studies, surveys, and other projects have highlighted the need for enhanced career services for doctoral students. These studies note the mismatch between students' academic training and potential career paths, underscored by a tight academic job market and the challenges these students face in the transition to other employment options (Golde and Dore, 2001; Washington University, 2003; Woodrow Wilson National Fellowship Foundation, 2004). This section provides a backdrop of the most salient career development needs of these students and the role to be played by career services.

The Population Defined. This section focuses on students who are in academically focused programs, whose presumed career path is primarily in teaching or research. This definition includes Ph.D. students at every stage of the degree process and students engaged in research master's programs. One important characteristic of this population, albeit a generalization, is that students often enroll in these types of degree programs "without considering a full range of alternatives and without developing a clear understanding of why they are doing so" (Golde and Dore, 2001, p. 21). This lack of purpose can have a significant impact on students' future career development.

Salient Career Issues. Doctoral and research master's students face a number of career issues:

• *Exposure to career options.* Students in academically oriented programs need more exposure to a wider variety of career options. The "At Cross Purposes" report identified "considerable evidence that there are far more job seekers than there are tenure-track jobs available, and that this structural imbalance, rather than temporary, is the new status quo" (Golde and Dore, 2001, p. 18). The report goes on to state that even graduates who find academic positions will quite likely work at institutions for which they have little exposure or specific training. This study indicates that students are not prepared for the labor market realities they face on finishing their academic careers, both within and outside the academy.

• *Nonacademic career exploration.* Our own experiences, and those from colleagues around the country, indicate that students have varying levels of experience and exposure to nonacademic career fields. One physics doctoral student interested in a career in investment banking might have audited a class in finance and done an internship, while another might have absolutely no knowledge of the industry. Departments, with their focus on academic pursuits, are often not positioned to help students connect with employers outside the academic realm (Woodrow Wilson National Fellowship Foundation, 2004). The employment contacts that can make an important difference to students in professional programs might not exist in academic departments. Students who have had exposure to the linear, somewhat rigid

New Directions for Student Services • DOI: 10.1002/ss

career paths of academe might easily feel overwhelmed by the less structured options outside the academy.

• *Job search support.* Whether pursuing academic or nonacademic options, students increasingly need support in reaching their goals. The tight academic market places a premium on the strongest application materials, the well-schooled interviewee, and the savvy job searcher. Students looking outside the academy feel the pressures to redefine their skills and experiences in ways that are meaningful to a more diverse set of employers and to make sense of a variety of job search strategies. Furthermore, although students might have the necessary skills for nonacademic positions, they likely need support in adapting those skills to the employment setting (LaPidus, 1998).

• *Transitions from graduate school.* The emotional issues related to leaving graduate school should not be underestimated. Even students who receive academic employment face disillusionment if the first postgraduate opportunity is not the ideal job (Stewart, 1995). Those leaving the academy potentially face even more difficult issues. A student whose identity has been tightly framed by the academic experience for many years might confront feelings of loss or failure as she or he tries to make sense of a new professional identity (Kajatani and Bryant, 2005).

The career concerns we have listed in many ways present the most complex or challenging issues students face. The reality is that these students, incredibly bright and armed with highly sought skills and experiences, do find satisfying jobs and careers in a variety of fields. Career services, however, can help students expand their perceptions of available career options and prepare for a broad range of positions.

The Role of Career Services. The following key career services can help students with career planning and decision making and also in implementing their plans:

• *Career counseling and advising.* Individualized service is extremely useful for Ph.D. students. Because of the complex issues many of these students face, counseling and advising provide individual attention to help ensure that students' needs are being met. Counseling must be confidential, especially for students pursuing nonacademic careers, since these students might fear negative consequences if advisors discover they are pursuing career goals outside the academy. Students will also benefit if counseling staff have had training on issues related to working with doctoral students.

• *Programming.* Workshops and programs are a safe way for many students to begin working with career services. Group work helps students understand that they are not alone in dealing with career issues; experience shows that graduate students are very supportive and can be helpful resources and sounding boards for one another. Programming can be useful for many academic job search topics, such as preparing written materials, interviewing, understanding different types of positions and different types of employers, and dual-career-couple issues. In addition to many of the basic topics, such as résumé writing and interviewing preparation, programming on nonacademic topics also should include opportunities for Ph.D. students to connect with professionals currently working in fields of interest. Students can gain important firsthand perspective from these connections. Traditionally academic units have not focused on developing relationships with employers (Woodrow Wilson National Fellowship Foundation, 2004). Career services, however, typically do foster these types of relationships.

• *Placement services.* Traditional placement services such as job fairs and on-campus recruiting have varying degrees of effectiveness for Ph.D. students. Employers who use these services are often most focused on hiring at the bachelor's degree level. As a result, Ph.D. students may need to take the initiative to find the most effective ways to connect with recruiters, and career services staff can help students understand how to use these services effectively. Students should be prepared to translate their academic skills and experiences for employers and to counter any misperceptions or stereotypes recruiters might have about those with doctorates.

Providing comprehensive, ongoing career services allows career professionals to have a regular presence in the lives of students. Promoting these resources on a regular basis, to both students and academic administrators, will help students feel comfortable engaging in their own career development throughout their academic career.

Working with Master's Students

Professional master's programs offer exposure, training, and experience leading to work in specific professions. Theses programs cover a wide range of fields that tend to be grouped in the social sciences (for example, education, public policy, social work, and urban planning), sciences (for example, natural resources and environment), and engineering. (For this chapter, we are generally excluding students in business, law, and medical schools. The needs of these students are distinctive. Students tend to benefit from career services that are tailored specifically to those needs.)

Salient Factors That Affect Career Services. Despite representing a diversity of fields, the academic departments and the students in these programs do tend to share some common traits and issues that can affect how career services are provided:

• *Orientation to a profession.* Academic departments and students in these programs tend to be oriented toward groups of standard career areas or professions, although some students will deviate from these standards for a variety of reasons. Students who complete these programs might reasonably expect to have had the training and experiences that can further their professional careers in substantial ways, usually targeting specific career fields. Most programs have strong affiliations with the professions their field represents through associations, employers, and other organizations. As a general rule, the academic unit might offer some career services to its students, although these services can take many forms and can vary in degree of development (Weidman, Twale and Stein, 2001).

• *Professional identity issues.* Master's programs place significant emphasis on the development of professional identity, that is, joining a community of professionals (Weidman, Twale, and Stein, 2001). Students whose career goals do not mesh with the norms of their graduate programs might struggle with issues of professional identity compared with their peers. These students might feel as though they made the wrong choice of graduate programs and, as a result, might explore alternative career options.

• *Reasons for pursuing a degree.* Students enter professional degree programs for a variety of reasons that have implications for career services (Anderson, 1998). Some pursue a degree as a credential needed to begin a career in a field or perhaps as an important step in the process of career advancement. For some, a master's degree constitutes an extension of work studied as an undergraduate, for others a next-best alternative to a doctorate. Understanding a student's reasons for choosing a master's program and how that reasoning changes during graduate school can provide important insights into working with individual students. There also might be significant differences between students who are attending a master's program immediately after their undergraduate degree and those who have taken some time between degrees.

The Role of Career Services. By the end of a degree program, as students make the transition to the professional world, they should be able to answer some key questions: How do I employ the skills I have developed? How do I define myself in relation to my chosen profession? How do others perceive me as a professional (Weidman, Twale, and Stein, 2001)? Career services can help students find their own answers and realize their professional identity. Services offered include career counseling, traditional placement services, and alumni and networking resources.

• *Career counseling.* Professional master's students, in part because of their status between the baccalaureate degree and the doctorate, can benefit from traditional career counseling and advising services. Often their concerns and issues are very similar to those of undergraduates: exploring options, making career decisions, and job searching. Career services staff bring the expertise and experience to work effectively with these students. In other ways, these students bring experiences and perspectives that are different from the undergraduate experience (Anderson, 1998). The individualized nature of career counseling can be a good environment to address more complex and specific issues. Career services staff can benefit from specific training to help them understand the unique issues that professional master's students face in the career planning process.

• *Traditional placement services.* Master's students can be active users of many of the traditional placement resources offered on campus. Tools such as job fairs and on-campus interviewing offer connections to employers in a wide variety of fields. Career services can also partner with academic units to develop employment opportunities that meet the needs of students with specific graduate training. Placement and recruiting resources may be offered directly through academic units, especially with employers who have very specific hiring needs.

• *Alumni and networking resources.* Networking opportunities can be especially helpful for master's students as part of the career exploration and job search process. Alumni who have become fully socialized into a profession are useful role models. Networking sources should ideally be a part of the educational process from the earliest stages of a student's academic career, contributing to the professional socialization process.

Conclusion

Graduate and professional students are a significant part of campus communities that need and deserve career services designed to help them reach their professional and personal goals. In a labor market and economy that increasingly demands high-level skill sets, graduate and professional students are prepared to add value to a broad range of organizations within the academy and beyond. Career development staff and services integrated throughout students' experiences can help ensure that graduate students are making thoughtful and intentional career decisions as they make the transition to a professional path following graduate school.

References

Anderson, M. S. (ed.). *The Experience of Being in Graduate School: An Exploration.* New Directions for Higher Education, no. 101. San Francisco: Jossey-Bass, 1998.

Golde, C. M., and Dore, T. M. "At Cross Purposes: What the Experiences of Today's Doctoral Students Reveal About Doctoral Education." 2001. Retrieved Aug. 30, 2005, from http://www.phd-survey.org.

Kajatani, M. P., and Bryant, R. A. "A Ph.D. and a Failure." *Chronicle of Higher Education,* Mar. 24, 2005. Retrieved Aug. 30, 2005, from http://chronicle.com/jobs/news/2005/03/2005032401c/careers.html.

Kroll, J., and Rentz, A. "Career Planning and Placement." In A. Rentz and G. Saddlemire (eds.), *Student Affairs Functions in Higher Education.* Springfield, Ill.: Charles C. Thomas, 1988.

LaPidus, J. B. "Doctoral Education and Student Career Needs." In A. S. Pruitt-Logan and P. D. Isaac (eds.), *Student Services for the Changing Graduate Student Population.* New Directions for Student Services, no. 72. San Francisco: Jossey-Bass, 1995.

LaPidus, J. B. "If We Want Things to Stay as They Are, Things Will Have to Change." In M. S. Anderson (ed.), *The Experience of Being in Graduate School: An Exploration.* New Directions for Higher Education, no. 101. San Francisco: Jossey-Bass, 1998.

Luzzo, D. A. "Career Development of Returning-Adult and Graduate Students." In D. A. Luzzo (ed.), *Career Counseling of College Students.* Washington, D.C.: American Psychological Association, 2000.

Nerad, M., and Miller, D. S. "Increasing Student Retention in Graduate and Professional Programs." In J. Grant Haworth (ed.), *Assessing Graduate and Professional Education: Current Realities, Future Prospects.* New Directions for Institutional Research, no. 92. San Francisco: Jossey-Bass, 1996.

Nyquist, J., and Wulff, D. H. "Re-envisioning the Ph.D.: Recommendations from National Studies on Doctoral Education." University of Washington, 2000. Retrieved Aug. 29, 2005, from http://www.grad.washington.edu/envision/project_resources/national_recommend.html.

Stewart, D. W. "Developmental Considerations in Counseling Graduate Students." *Guidance and Counseling,* 1995, *10*(3), 21–23.

Washington University. *Proceedings of the National Conference on Graduate Student Leadership.* St. Louis, Mo.: Washington University, 2003.

Weidman, J. C., and Stein, E. L. "Socialization of Doctoral Students to Academic Norms." *Research in Higher Education,* 2003, *44*(7), 641–656.

Weidman, J. C., Twale, D. J., and Stein, E. L. *Socialization of Graduate and Professional Students in Higher Education.* ASHE-ERIC Higher Education Report, vol. 28, no. 3. San Francisco: Jossey-Bass, 2001.

Woodrow Wilson National Fellowship Foundation. "WRK4US Discussion List." 2000. Retrieved Aug. 11, 2005, from http://www.woodrow.org/phd/WRK4US/.

Woodrow Wilson National Fellowship Foundation. "Responsive Ph.D.: Agenda." 2004. Retrieved Aug. 10, 2005, from http://www.woodrow.org/responsivephd/agenda.html.

TOM LEHKER *is senior assistant director for graduate student services at the University of Michigan's Career Center.*

JENNIFER S. FURLONG *is a career counselor for graduate students and postdoctoral fellows at the University of Pennsylvania.*

7

Defined as space, programs, staff, and involved students, graduate student centers build community among and create engagement for graduate students while also providing necessary services. This chapter explores the potential of graduate student centers to improve graduate education.

Graduate Student Centers: Building Community and Involving Students

Lisa C. O. Brandes

In the past ten years, many doctoral universities, both extensive and intensive, have built, or proposed building, graduate student centers to serve their graduate and professional (G/P) students. In this chapter, I define graduate student centers and discuss the range of their configurations, services and functions. I illustrate these ideas with a case study of the McDougal Graduate Student Center, a comprehensive center for student life and professional development at Yale University.

What Is a Graduate Student Center?

Over the past decade, the actual and planned construction of specialized centers for graduate and professional students has grown significantly. A number of public and private doctoral universities have established graduate student centers and graduate programming offices (Table 7.1). Many more doctoral institutions are studying, lobbying, or preparing for a graduate student center (Table 7.2). Most graduate student centers have existed less than ten years (examples are Stanford, University of California at Santa Cruz, and Yale), although a few began much earlier, often as residential centers (for example, Princeton's Graduate College).

Currently, no single definition of a standard graduate student center exists. A general characterization is necessary, however, to provide a framework for discussing and describing structures and functions of such centers. For purposes of this chapter, a graduate student center includes

NEW DIRECTIONS FOR STUDENT SERVICES, no. 115, Fall 2006   © Wiley Periodicals, Inc.
Published online in Wiley InterScience (www.interscience.wiley.com) • DOI: 10.1002/ss.218

Table 7.1. Graduate Student Centers and Program Offices: Examples

Comprehensive or Multipurpose Graduate Centers	Graduate Centers with a Significant Residential Component
Boston College: Murray House	Massachusetts Institute of Technology: Sidney-Pacific Graduate Community
Cornell University: Big Red Barn Graduate Center	Ohio State University: South Campus Gateway
Harvard University: Dudley House	Princeton University: The Graduate College
University of Michigan: Rackham	University of California, Berkeley: Ida Louise Jackson Graduate House
Savannah College of Art and Design: Graduate Studies Center at Smithfield Cottage	Virginia Polytechnic Institute: Graduate Life Center at Donaldson Brown
Stanford University: Graduate Community Center	
Syracuse University: Inn Complete Graduate Student Center	
University of British Columbia: Thea Koerner House	
University of California, Santa Cruz: Graduate Commons	
University of California, San Francisco: Graduate Student Center	
University of Pennsylvania: Graduate Student Center	
Yale University: McDougal Graduate Student Center	

Modest Graduate Student Lounges or Rooms in Campus Centers or Academic Buildings	Graduate Student Life or Activities Program Offices Without a Multipurpose Center
Arizona State University	Brandeis University
Brown University	Dartmouth College
Columbia University	Massachusetts Institute of Technology
Lehigh University	Montclair State University
Long Island University	University of Maryland
University of Maine	
Michigan Technological University	
University of Oklahoma	
Rutgers University	
Trinity International University	
University of California, Los Angeles	
Kentucky University	
University of New England	
University of North Carolina	

Note: This table does not include so-called graduate student centers that house only admissions, registrar, or academic affairs offices, without significant student activities or professional development services. It also excludes centers that provide only online information.

Source: Compiled through professional associations, Internet searches, and inspection of institutional Web pages as of August 2005.

NEW DIRECTIONS FOR STUDENT SERVICES • DOI: 10.1002/ss

Table 7.2. Toward a Graduate Center: Campus Reports, Surveys, and Advocacy by Students and Administrators to Build a Graduate Student Center

Arizona State University	Northeastern University
Columbia University	Northwestern University
University of Connecticut	University of Notre Dame
Dartmouth College	Radford University
Duke University	Rensselaer Polytechnic Institute
Emory University	University of California at Irvine
Florida State University	University of San Diego
Georgia Institute of Technology	University of Texas
Indiana University	Trinity International University
University of Maryland	University of Virginia
New York University	University of Waikato (New Zealand)
University of Nevada-Reno	Washington University, St. Louis
	Western Michigan University

Note: This table does not include so-called graduate student centers that house only admissions, registrar, or academic affairs offices, without significant student activities or professional development services. It also excludes centers that provide only online information.

Source: Compiled through professional associations, Internet searches, and inspection of institutional Web pages as of August 2005.

graduate student space, specialized graduate student services and programs, graduate student affairs staff, and professionals or involved graduate students.

Graduate Student Space. A graduate student center entails a building or multiple rooms dedicated to serving graduate and professional students. G/P students express interest in centers with spaces to socialize, study, host seminars, group meetings, and conferences, and engage in organized student activities.

Existing graduate student centers, and institutional proposals calling for the development of such centers, include amenities tailored to meet the needs and interests of the campus graduate community: well-equipped meeting rooms; lounges with tables and chairs for studying and comfortable furniture for socializing; a dining hall, café, or coffee bar, and perhaps even a pub; recreation or game rooms, with TVs, game tables, and board games; a children's area for G/P student parents; a music practice or performance room; offices for graduate student center or student life programming staff; graduate student government offices; a box office selling tickets for center-sponsored events and off-campus venues; and general facilities such as e-mail kiosks, computer rooms with printers and copiers, wired and wireless Internet access, telephones, bulletin boards, and information racks.

NEW DIRECTIONS FOR STUDENT SERVICES • DOI: 10.1002/ss

The desired space needs suggest the creation of a sizable graduate student center. Facilities and financial resource limitations at many institutions, however, preclude the creation of such a space. As a starting point, a simple lounge or room in a campus center, designated specifically for graduate students, might contain some of these functions and basic services. Graduate student center space generally is distinct from undergraduate-centered spaces and mainly is nonresidential, open to G/P students regardless of where they live. At many institutions, the majority of G/P students live off-campus, with only a small number in on-campus residence halls or apartments. Nonresidential graduate student centers provide a home, or at least a living room, on campus for students. Residentially based centers, such as Princeton or Virginia Polytechnic Institute, welcome nonresident G/Ps into their community. Buildings and rooms provide necessary gathering places for graduate students.

Space to Build Community. A specialized graduate student center space builds community for graduate students by providing a dedicated physical place for G/P students from different departments and academic programs to meet informally, study together, and organize student group activities. In fact, most existing graduate student centers and many student-led initiatives to create new centers expressly state community building as a mission or goal (see Tables 7.1 and 7.2).

Graduate students want and need to build their communities. In surveys, national samples of graduate students responded that they often felt little sense of community or connection to one another or to the larger university. They also reported wanting interdisciplinary opportunities to meet, socialize, share intellectually, and work with other students in different programs (Golde and Dore, 2001; Lovitts, 2001). A graduate student center space can serve these needs by providing a designated location where community building can occur.

As studies demonstrate and as anyone who has undertaken graduate study understands, the graduate school experience can be both intellectually challenging and socially isolating (Caple, 1995; Lovitts, 2001). Doctoral study, in particular, can be a time of intense solitude, especially in the non-lab social sciences and the humanities. Many graduate departments and doctoral programs offer little opportunity or incentive for students to meet or interact with others outside one's subdiscipline, lab group, or school. Interests, activities, and interactions become increasingly narrow as graduate students progress through their lengthy course of study, which may last five to seven years or more. Departmental and disciplinary culture might even increase this narrowing of students' outlook and sense of self (Golde and Dore, 2001; Lovitts, 2001).

In this environment, social integration on several levels is important to graduate student retention and degree completion. A multicampus attrition study found that "in general, the more opportunities for integration a student received, the more integrated the student became, and the more likely the student was to complete" (Lovitts, 2001, p. 100). To enhance student success, building community and social integration should be an important part of the graduate educational experience. With a graduate student center, students can engage in campus life and counteract the structural isolation and disconnectedness of the graduate experience. A graduate student center also operates as a safe or neutral space for students to explore a variety of personal or professional interests while escaping the pressures of the lab or library or disciplinary expectations, for a time. Such a center offers graduate students opportunities to make and talk with friends from various departments and professional schools or to discuss academic, personal, or family matters with professional staff members who are not part of their academic programs.

Space for community building across academic boundaries also holds potential for retaining and supporting diverse student populations, particularly women, international students, students of color, and lesbian, gay, bisexual, transgendered, or questioning (LGBTQ) students. Many graduate departments and degree programs lack diversity or a critical mass of women or students of color, for example. A graduate student center offers a place for potentially marginalized students across academic programs and departments to meet and share with students like themselves. Interdepartmental space and group-specific services and activities are particularly vital to the academic success and persistence of graduate students from groups still underrepresented in the academy (Cheatham and Phelps, 1995).

Space to Gather. A graduate student center space designed and run specifically for G/P students can be a visible sign that the institution values and cares about its graduate and professional students. Real estate, in a physical graduate student center, puts these students on the campus map, literally and symbolically.

While there may be an existing campus center or student union, it likely focuses mainly on undergraduate students in most of its activities. A separate space for graduate students is necessary to give G/Ps their own opportunities to learn outside the classroom. Graduate students want a place of their own on the university campus, and they want their name on it to know that they are welcome. The words "Graduate-Professional Student Center," rather than merely "Student Center," or "Graduate Student Career Services," rather than merely "Career Counseling," represent a critical welcome mat for G/P students.

As a common practice, graduate student center spaces are designated primarily or exclusively for use by the graduate and professional student population. It might be the case that anyone can eat at the center café or that undergraduates can meet with graduate teaching assistants holding office hours at the center. In a typical center, however, meeting rooms, computers, lounges, and other resources are reserved for G/P student use. A physical space designated specifically for G/P students invites students to enter and provides a home on campus, as well as structures and resources for establishing communities across academic programs and departments. Community building, however, requires more than physical space. Services and programming specific to graduate students are necessary to augment the opportunities that physical space can provide.

Graduate Student Services and Programming. Graduate and professional students have enrolled at research/doctoral university campuses in large numbers for some time. At some doctoral extensive universities, for example, the number of graduate M.A., Ph.D., and professional students equals or exceeds the number of undergraduate students. Despite their numbers, many G/Ps experience centralized campus student services as designed mainly for undergraduate students. Indeed, a widespread assumption among student affairs professionals is that academic departments or faculty advisors address G/P students' academic, personal, and professional needs. However, academic departments and graduate student interests often are at cross-purposes with regard to professional development and student needs (Golde and Dore, 2001).

Surveyed doctoral students, for instance, wanted wide-ranging intellectual experiences, practical guidance for varied career options, and strong pedagogical training, services that their departments generally did not provide or encourage them to pursue. As noted earlier, Ph.D. students felt pressure to narrow their academic focus or curtail personal interests. Their disciplinary cultures rarely promoted a conception of the well-rounded student or balanced individual, instead valuing the single-minded scholar (Lovitts, 2001).

The central academic administration of graduate schools might not have trained staff or resources to provide the range of necessary graduate student services. Increasingly, however, the higher education community has recognized the importance of specialized student services for those pursuing graduate and professional degrees, with distinct G/P services necessary in such areas as career counseling, teacher training, international student support, mental health, and social life (Committee on Science, Engineering, and Public Policy, 1995; Pruitt-Logan and Isaac, 1995; Golde and Dore, 2001; Lovitts, 2001). Within student affairs, the recent American College Personnel Association and National Association of Student Personnel Administrators white paper *Learning Reconsidered* calls for "a new campus emphasis at comprehensive institutions on the graduate student experience" and urges "creating graduate student affairs support systems" (2004, p. 22). This joint association white paper directs student affairs professionals to provide resources and services specifically for G/P students.

Other chapters in this volume demonstrate the potential for focused student services to meet the changing needs of graduate and professional students. This section concentrates on student life and professional development programs as practiced at existing graduate student centers. Items discussed include general student services, student life programs and activities, professional development opportunities, and collaboration with other campus offices and programs.

NEW DIRECTIONS FOR STUDENT SERVICES • DOI: 10.1002/ss

General Graduate Student Services. A well-designed graduate student center offers students "one-stop shopping" for relevant information, services, and referrals. Such a center can serve as a centralized distribution point, both physically and online, for information about and services related to academic topics such as advising or course discussions, personal topics such as financial aid or child care, professional development topics such as research presentation opportunities or career development, and interpersonal topics such as social events and student organizations.

The range of student services offered by existing graduate student centers includes advising and support of graduate student organizations and student governments; assisting with admissions and recruitment efforts through tours, open houses, publications, and Web sites; coordinating schoolwide or universitywide orientation programs for new G/Ps; organizing graduation activities; participating in or hosting graduate alumni and alumnae activities; and producing communications, Web resources, and information designed for G/P students.

Student Life Programs and Activities. Graduate student centers can provide important opportunities for graduate students to interact with one another as well as faculty and student affairs professionals. Student life programs, services, and activities offered through graduate student centers include graduate student social activities, such as pub nights, dances, coffeehouses, and barbecues, where G/P students meet one another outside labs, studios, or classes; interdisciplinary intellectual events, such as current events talks, guest lectures, student group discussions, and student-faculty research conferences; arts and cultural outings and student performances; sports events and intramural competitions, as well as fitness and wellness sessions; stress management workshops and mental health information; crafts, yoga, and other enrichment classes; cultural celebrations and multicultural activities; community service opportunities; and events tailored specifically to meet the needs of women, international students, students of color, LGBTQ students, and G/P student families.

Professional Development Programs. Institutions increasingly provide professional development programs for many graduate and professional students. Professional development programs offered include graduate career services such as counseling, job search workshops, and programs for exploring a wide range of career options; teacher training; mentoring and advising programs for faculty and students, especially for marginalized populations; writing workshops and dissertation groups; fellowship and grant-writing seminars; seminars on the ethical conduct of research; foreign language conversation groups; and English as-a-second-language courses.

Collaboration with Other Offices. The graduate student center might not produce directly all of the described services. Often the graduate student center and other student affairs offices will collaborate to provide necessary services for G/P students. For example, to reach the G/P population,

NEW DIRECTIONS FOR STUDENT SERVICES • DOI: 10.1002/ss

a graduate student counselor from the campus career center might hold programs or office hours at the center or publicize services directly through the center newsletter or e-mail list.

Graduate student centers can enhance the services provided to G/P students by working with specific degree programs and faculty members. Centers might partner with graduate faculty on services hosted in departments, especially for teaching, academic careers, and writing. Discipline-specific programs might include a history academic job search workshop, a chemistry teaching seminar, or a bioscience National Science Foundation grant workshop. Where the departments are large and the faculty willing, department-centered program collaboration is possible; in other cases, combining students from smaller, related departments for general, academically relevant programs might prove more useful. Regardless of the format, collaboration with other offices, staff, and faculty can bolster the services provided for graduate and professional students.

Graduate Student Affairs Professionals. Along with space and specific programs, an effective graduate student center requires dedicated professionals to plan its programs and serve the needs of G/P students. Recognizing the need for and benefits of such staff, a number of institutions have hired student affairs professionals to serve their students. Other leading public and private research institutions are debating, planning, or wishing for centers, services, and specific student affairs professionals to work with G/P students (see Tables 7.1 and 7.2).

Graduate center directors, graduate student affairs deans, or graduate student life directors are among the new positions created in the past decade to serve the needs and interests of graduate and professional students. Growth in the area of graduate student affairs led the National Association of Student Personnel Administrators (NASPA) to establish a new networking group, Administrators in Graduate and Professional Student Services. Other formal and informal associations for graduate career counselors, teaching center directors, and graduate student center directors have developed as graduate student affairs professionals search for colleagues across the nation.

The administrative structures for graduate student affairs professionals vary in visibility, independence, collaboration, reporting relationships, and student populations served. Four major staffing practices exist at research institutions, each with different implications for graduate student centers.

In the first staffing practice, a graduate school houses an assistant or associate dean of student affairs, director of graduate student services, or a director of the graduate center (Yale, Montclair State, and Harvard are examples). The person ultimately reports to the graduate school dean and has strong school support, opportunities for collaboration with academic administrators and graduate faculty, and good credibility with students and academic departments. A graduate school–based staff member might not easily serve a large professional student population, however, unless the pro-

New Directions for Student Services • DOI: 10.1002/ss

grams or center are open to and targeted toward interested G/P students. With this structure, the graduate school student affairs professional must actively build cooperative working relationships with other campus student services providers, such as housing offices or health services.

In the second structure, a graduate student life director or assistant or associate dean is part of a student affairs division, often with an indirect reporting line or a strong working relationship with the graduate or professional school deans' offices (Boston College and the University of Maryland use this structure). Where a centralized student affairs division exists, it can simply appoint a graduate student affairs specialist. For this staff member, the main challenges come in building relationships with the schools, degree programs, and G/P students they seek to serve.

In the third general practice, a graduate student center exists under the provost or vice president for research (as at the University of Pennsylvania). This practice works where the center serves all G/P students, as at Penn, or where there is no graduate school but instead a collection of independent colleges and schools administering their own graduate programs. Challenges for this staff member likely include working with many supervisors and serving G/P students with varied needs and differing degree program structures spread across the campus.

Finally, in relatively rare cases, a student affairs professional works for a graduate student council or government. This structure typically exists only where a graduate student association has great independence and often significant funding, usually from student fees (examples are the University of Nevada at Reno and MIT). In their recent strategic plan, however, even the powerful University of Nevada at Reno graduate student association proposed moving the staff member fully into the employ of the graduate school and separating the services office and staff from the student association (Graduate Student Assembly, 2005).

Although each staffing structure presents its own benefits and challenges in serving graduate and professional students, the important element of each is the presence of a student affairs professional dedicated to working with G/P students.

Involved Graduate Students Graduate Student Assembly. While dedicated space, varied programs, and student affairs professionals are important, involved students can be the crucial element in graduate student center program success and student satisfaction. First, by their very existence and operation, graduate student centers have the potential to foster student engagement. A rich array of student organizations and strong student governments can result from the space, services, and staff found with active graduate student centers. In addition, many centers, both new and well established, rely on paid or volunteer peer programmers. These involved graduate student leaders organize events and services of interest to the G/P student community. This section discusses general G/P involvement and the role of center peer programmers.

Building Involvement. A graduate student center constitutes a powerful resource for building community among graduate students and for enhancing student engagement with the institution. When created to be student centered and student led, a center directly involves graduate students in providing needed programs while promoting student involvement in general. Through involvement with a graduate student center, either in program participation or planning, the potential exists for previously isolated G/P students to become further engaged with and feel a part of the university.

Over the course of a two- to seven-year period of study, centers offer graduate students many different means of engaging with one another. G/Ps can socialize with students from different disciplines, share in campus celebrations, hear distinguished faculty lecture, attend sporting or arts events, meet senior administrators, network with noted alumni and alumnae, dance at student parties, or find support in thesis and dissertation groups. Participation in common university traditions and experiences can provide outcomes associated with active engagement (see Chapter Four, this volume). Active involvement outside the degree department also helps G/P students identify themselves as part of the larger university. A student, for instance, might identify not only as a history student but also as a graduate student, a Yale University student, or a member of a student interest group. Each instance provides students with opportunities to build community and be involved with both curricular and co-curricular activities.

Involved Student Leaders. Students seeking even more involvement might work at the center, organizing events such as orientation or teacher training workshops, or serving as graduate council officers. This involvement provides leadership development opportunities for the G/P students engaged in planning activities for the center.

Many established graduate student centers involve the very G/P students they serve by using volunteer or paid graduate student program leaders. Who better to provide ideas, enthusiasm, and outreach for programs and to serve their peers than graduate and professional students themselves? Graduate students might serve as peer programmers, teaching consultants, or writing tutors, for instance. Since their center roles rarely relate directly to their graduate field of study or future careers, these students involve themselves at graduate student centers for purposes of enrichment, involvment, social interest, and service, as an addition to their academic pursuits in the laboratory or classroom.

In some cases, graduate student government officers are volunteer leaders, and occasionally they organize programs and services through a graduate student center. Officers and committee chairs can take responsibility for social programming (as at the University of Pennsylvania) or orientation (as at Massachusetts Institute of Technology). In other cases, the students helping plan center activities receive modest compensation, such as a small stipend, free room, or meal compensation. They also might have a special title, such as "fellow" at the graduate student centers at Harvard, Yale, and Penn.

A professional working with these paraprofessionals or student volunteers faces issues of recruitment, selection, mentoring, teamwork, motivation, and leadership development. Keeping these involved center peer leaders satisfied, on task, and able to balance extracurricular and academic life is a significant challenge to a staff member. Involving students has great rewards for the individuals, the quality of the activities produced, and the overall nature of the graduate experience for the community.

The McDougal Graduate Student Center at Yale: A Case Example

The McDougal Graduate Center at Yale developed over the course of the past ten years. This center provides an excellent illustration of how student space, specific student life and professional development services, professional directors, and intensive student involvement have dramatically changed the nature of the graduate school experience at Yale.

In 1995, the Yale Graduate School administration consisted of academic, financial aid, registration, and admissions staff serving about twenty-four hundred mostly doctoral students. Issues of funding doctoral study with adequate stipends and tuition fellowships, time to degree, and comprehensive health care coverage were contentious.

At that time, the average Yale Ph.D. student received almost no centralized professional development or student life services and experienced little community outside, and sometimes inside, his or her departments. No career counseling was available. A small group of graduate students ran a simple teacher training program. Until graduation day, graduate students participated in almost no schoolwide events after the brief orientation session their first day. With no graduate student council, few interdepartmental student organizations, and limited schoolwide communications, student involvement outside class or department was limited. In general, Yale graduate students, like those at comparable private and public doctoral institutions, felt isolated, underserved, and ill equipped for teaching and future careers.

In this environment, a concerned graduate school dean made plans to increase student financial support and create a graduate student center. With support from senior university officers, in 1996, Dean Thomas Appelquist found a generous alumnus, Alfred McDougal '53, and his wife, Nancy Lauter, both of whom shared his vision for a center involving and serving graduate students. A Yale planning group gave the new McDougal Center space, services, staff, and student involvement using Harvard University's relatively new Dudley House Graduate Center as a benchmark.

Space. The planning group of students, faculty, administrators, and alumni and alumnae recommended restoring space in the existing Hall of

Graduate Studies (HGS), an architecturally distinctive building in the center of the Yale campus, to serve as the space for the McDougal Graduate Student Center. HGS houses the Graduate School administration, several graduate departments, a graduate dormitory, and a dining hall. A graduate student center was seen as a natural complement to the building. When the renovated McDougal Center space officially opened in fall 1997, students had access to the restored neogothic Common Room lounge, a student-run café, a large meeting room, staff offices, and work spaces. With two minor renovations, the center now contains a resource library, upgraded media equipment in the heavily used meeting room, a box office, and a basement level with a recreation room, kids' corner, computer cluster, music room, and more offices. Graduate students can use center facilities weekdays from 9:00 A.M. to 11:00 P.M. and weekends from 11:00 A.M. to 11:00 P.M. during the academic year, with shorter hours in summer.

Services and Programs. In the first years, small but growing numbers of students participated in the schoolwide, student-initiated programs such as movies, social hours, and recreational trips. Today graduate students and their families attend a wide range of student life activities, from arts to sports to children's events. Most student life events are free or, if ticketed, sold at cost. Professional development programs include comprehensive career services, a teaching center, and writing and mentoring programs. While some services focus on the needs of doctoral and masters students in the Graduate School, postdoctoral fellows and professional school students are welcome to attend many programs.

Having a comprehensive graduate student center allows Yale to provide services to build community from preadmission to postgraduation. Departments receive assistance with recruitment, and admitted students receive their transition information and orientation programs through the center. Instead of the previous two-hour orientation session, new students now participate in a week of orientation activities designed to introduce the Graduate School, the university, various campus services, and the community of New Haven. The McDougal Center coordinates and hosts graduate school commencement activities as well so that students begin and end their Yale graduate study at their center. The goal, and the expected effect, is to provide an integrated and holistic network of co-curricular and extracurricular support services for graduate students throughout their course of study and as alums.

Staff. In 1996–1997, the McDougal Center began with one professional staff member, a director of student life, in a temporary office during renovations. The center now is a comprehensive graduate student center with offices of student life, careers, and teaching, each led by a professional director and four additional professional and support staff. Based on committee recommendations and student interest, Yale appointed new center directors of career services and teacher training in the initial years. All three directors report to the dean of the graduate school and enjoy significant independence in providing programming. As assistant dean for student affairs and director of student life in the McDougal Center, for example, I work with individual students, student groups, faculty members, and, in an extremely decentralized student services environment, varied campus departments, as a coordinator of graduate student services.

Student Involvement. Graduate students who use the facilities, services, and programs of the Yale graduate student center benefit from out-of-class involvement. The mission of the McDougal Center, like other sister graduate centers, is to be a student involvement center run by, for, and with graduate students. Peer programmers, student government officers, and student group leaders are crucial to the center's ability to serve student interests.

The McDougal Center fellows contribute immensely to the success and reach of the center. Their roles and numbers have grown. In the first year, four McDougal graduate fellows planned the initial student life activities. Now, eight years into the existence of the McDougal Center, nearly twenty fellows each year organize programs in arts and music, academic writing, career development, community service, social events, sports, wellness, and women's mentoring. Teams of fellows produce an award-winning literary magazine, *Palimpsest*; provide family events; and manage the Blue Dog Café. About fifteen graduate teaching center fellows also organize a variety of pedagogical workshops and services annually. Both teams of fellows provide opportunities for engagement and leadership through student team coordinators, intensive training, structured meetings, and distinct responsibilities for program planning, implementation, and evaluation.

Also created in 1997, the Graduate Student Assembly meets and has offices in the McDougal Center. The assembly has developed strong working relationships with school administrators, achieved some notable policy gains, and led its own initiatives over the years. Finally, from one graduate student group in 1998, the student life office now registers, advises, and supports over twenty-five groups annually. Involved students at every level are the lifeblood of this graduate center.

Building a Center, Building a Dream

Some university administrators might worry that any graduate student center is a waste of space and money, despite the benefits described in this chapter. Some campus officials, in fact, have argued that graduate students will not leave the library or laboratory to regularly use the facility or its services (see, for example, Walker, 2001). At Yale, some faculty, and even some students, expressed skepticism initially, as well.

Can student affairs professionals use a graduate student center with space, services, and involved students to build community from the isolated graduate experience? The experience of existing graduate centers demonstrates that it is possible. In particular, at the McDougal Center, graduate students do come, often in large numbers. Each of the various student life and professional development events attracts from a dozen to several hundred G/P students and postdoctoral fellows from departments and schools across the Yale campus.

Rather than standing empty, the McDougal meeting rooms are in constant use for center and school programs and also for student organizations, conferences, and study groups. Center meeting rooms are booked regularly during lunchtime, afternoons, evenings, and many weekends. To meet growing student demand for space in their graduate student center, the Common Room has added tables not once but twice. Yale built it, and graduate students come to use the center to create their own graduate community.

Conclusion

Graduate student centers can be critical tools for building community among graduate students. Centers incorporating space, services, staff, and involved students offer opportunities for interaction across disciplines, enhanced engagement, and leadership opportunities. These elements provide a framework for institutions to create new centers or improve existing ones. Of the 261 institutions classified as doctoral extensive or intensive (Carnegie Foundation for the Advancement of Teaching, 2000), only a small number have multipurpose graduate centers. Given the number of campuses engaged in discussions of establishing a center, the development of new graduate student centers likely will continue. Student affairs professionals can, and should, use such centers to better meet the needs, and enhance the experiences, of graduate students.

References

American College Personnel Association and National Association of Student Personnel Administrators. *Learning Reconsidered: A Campus-Wide Focus on the Student Experience.* Washington, D.C.: American College Personnel Association and National Association of Student Personnel Administrators, 2004.

Caple, R. B. "Counseling Graduate Students." In A. S. Pruitt-Logan and P. D. Isaac (eds.), *Student Services for the Changing Graduate Student Population.* New Directions for Student Services, no. 42. San Francisco: Jossey-Bass, 1995.

Carnegie Foundation for the Advancement of Teaching. "The Carnegie Classification of Institutions of Higher Education." Stanford, Calif.: Carnegie Foundation for the Advancement of Teaching, 2000. Retrieved July 20, 2005, from http://www. carnegiefoundation.org/Classification/CIHE2000/Tables.htm.

Cheatham, H. E., and Phelps, C. "Promoting the Development of Graduate Students of Color." In A. S. Pruitt-Logan and P. D. Isaac (eds.), *Student Services for the Changing Graduate Student Population.* New Directions for Student Services, no. 42. San Francisco: Jossey-Bass, 1995.

Committee on Science, Engineering, and Public Policy. *Reshaping the Graduate Education of Scientists and Engineers.* Washington, D.C.: National Academy of Sciences, National Academy Press, 1995.

Golde, C. M., and Dore, T. M. "At Cross Purposes: What the Experiences of Today's Doctoral Students Reveal About Doctoral Education." 2001. Retrieved Aug. 30, 2005, from http://www.phd-survey.org.

Graduate Student Assembly, University of Texas, Austin. "A Resolution Calling for the Creation of a Graduate Student Center." Mar. 28, 2005. Retrieved July 20, 2005, from http://www.utexas.edu/studentgov/gsa/archives/legislation.php?type=GSA_BILL&id=369.

Lovitts, B. E. *Leaving the Ivory Tower: The Causes and Consequences of Departure from Doctoral Study.* Lanham, Md.: Rowman & Littlefield, 2001.

Pruitt-Logan, A. S., and Isaac, P. D. (eds.). *Student Services for the Changing Graduate Student Population.* New Directions for Student Services, no. 42. San Francisco: Jossey-Bass, 1995.

Walker, D. "Graduate Students Push for Specialized Center." *Diamondback Online.* College Park: University of Maryland, Nov. 13, 2001. Retrieved July 15, 2005, from http://www.diamondbackonline.com/News/Diamondback/archives/2001/11/13/news6.html.

Warner, R. "Feasibility Study for a Graduate and Professional Student Studies Center at the University of Virginia." In *Report of the Subcommittee on Quality of Life Issues, Academic Affairs Committee of the Faculty Senate.* Charlottesville: University of Virginia, Apr. 11, 2002. Retrieved July 15, 2005, from http://www.virginia.edu/facultysenate/warnerstudentctr.html.

LISA C. O. BRANDES *is assistant dean for student affairs and director of student life at the McDougal Graduate Student Center, Graduate School of Arts and Sciences, Yale University.*

NEW DIRECTIONS FOR STUDENT SERVICES • DOI: 10.1002/ss

8

Several common themes across chapters are discussed and implications for practice and research are offered.

Throwing Pebbles at Stonehenge: Advocating for Graduate and Professional Students

Melanie J. Guentzel, Becki Elkins Nesheim

One of the gratifying aspects of developing and editing a volume is the synergy created by bringing together authors from a variety of institutions and professional experiences. We sought to incorporate the bottom-up and insider perspectives on the needs of graduate and professional students and the services designed to address those needs. To that end, several authors are practitioners working with graduate and professional students in student services roles, and several are either current graduate students or recent graduates. All are passionate advocates for graduate and professional students. The chapters flowed from these authors' individual experiences. We were excited to find, then, several stated or implied commonalities across the chapters.

Common Themes

The themes that emerged across the chapters exemplify the need to consider how we can better serve graduate and professional students on our campuses. Taken as a collective, the chapters highlighted the need for (1) a safe or neutral space for graduate and professional students, (2) services designed specifically for graduate and professional students, (3) opportunities for students to interact across academic disciplines, (4) community building

NEW DIRECTIONS FOR STUDENT SERVICES, no. 115, Fall 2006   © Wiley Periodicals, Inc.
Published online in Wiley InterScience (www.interscience.wiley.com) • DOI: 10.1002/ss.219

among graduate and professional students, (5) academic and student affairs partnerships to provide appropriate services, and (6) assessment of student needs, satisfaction, and outcomes.

Safe or Neutral Spaces. Graduate and professional students need a safe or neutral space where they can receive information and explore identities and experiences beyond their department or discipline. Departments or professional schools are students' academic homes while they are pursuing their degrees, but they might not be a safe space for students. Students whose advisors are training them to be researchers might not be able to speak with them about a teaching career. Medical students might not be able to approach a peer or faculty member about their need for mental health services. Even if they are safe spaces for students, departments are rarely neutral places. A person, an office, even a Web site outside the department that provides information can go a long way toward easing student stress.

Services Designed Specifically for Graduate and Professional Students. A number of chapters identified the need for separate or specific services for graduate and professional students. Even when they are a significant portion of the campus population, graduate and professional students recognize that the campus belongs to undergraduates. In Chapter Seven, Lisa Brandes discussed the need to create separate graduate student centers, noting that space designated for the use of graduate and professional students is welcoming at a place centered on the undergraduate experience. In Chapter Six, Tom Lehker and Jennifer Furlong noted that graduate and professional students perceive institution career services as being for undergraduate students. Creating and publicizing a graduate career services office or position signals graduate and professional students that they are welcome and someone is available who can meet their needs.

Opportunities to Interact Across Disciplines. Educators and students must consider creating opportunities for students to interact across disciplines. One of the concerns of the reformers of undergraduate education is the fragmentation of the student experience. Students are not assisted in making the connection between disciplines or between academic knowledge and life skills. Graduate and professional education, because of the level of specialization, can be even more fragmented than the undergraduate experience. Student centers offering opportunities for social interaction as well as general professional development create spaces where students can get to know each other over shared involvements. Creating a space for students to build bridges across disciplines can generate a synergy of ideas that will improve the research conducted and ultimately improve undergraduate education.

Community Building. The idea of facilitating interdisciplinary interaction relates to our next theme of creating a community of graduate and professional students to counteract the isolation of graduate education. As Ann Gansemer-Topf, Leah Ewing Ross, and R. M. Johnson noted in Chapter Two, graduate and professional education focuses on the cognitive development of students—the life of the mind—while often neglecting the psychosocial needs of students. In addition, Chris Brus noted in Chapter Three on balance that creating community across the institution might be even more important for students of color, women, parents, older students, or others who may feel alone or marginalized in their departments. Graduate and professional education are challenging without the awareness that because of who you are, there is no one who can identify with or relate to your experience.

Academic and Student Affairs Partnerships. Throughout the chapters, it was clear that neither academic affairs nor student affairs can be solely responsible for graduate and professional student life. Partnership is needed to best serve this population. Chapter Five by Linda McGuire and Julie Phye, on the professional development of law and medical students, serves as an excellent example of the ways that faculty and student affairs professionals can work together to support a student's academic and professional development. Brus offered intervention recommendations for faculty, student affairs professionals, and students to break the attrition cycle for nontraditional graduate and professional students. Finally, Jason Pontius and Shaun Harper suggested in Chapter Four that in addition to orientation to the department, students need orientation to the institution as well. They suggest that academic schools and departments partner with student affairs to identify ways students can engage in out-of-class opportunities that support their in-class learning. Sharing responsibility for the experiences and learning of graduate and professional students will decrease the fragmentation of the student experience, as well as the isolation, and should enhance the student experience, improve social integration, and lower attrition rates.

Assessment. Many of the authors recognized and stated the need for assessment. Graduate and professional education, having largely escaped the calls for reform and accountability that have elicited the assessment movement in undergraduate education, has not widely engaged in the assessment of needs, experiences, and learning outcomes for graduate and professional education. Yet a glance at the research tells us that the problems and concerns that students encounter today, particularly with regard to attrition and degree completion, have been a persistent factor in graduate education (Atkinson, 1939; Austin, 2002; Katz and Hartnett, 1976; Pelikan, 1983; Rees, 1962). We need to conduct assessments to identify student needs, measure student satisfaction, and measure student learning outcomes. Our ability to provide appropriate services depends on the information garnered through such assessment.

Summary. The themes identified indicate that students experience graduate and professional education as fragmented and isolating and that the challenges of pursuing an advanced degree are not met with appropriate levels of support. Academic schools and departments are focused, appropriately, on the cognitive development and professional socialization of students. However, students do not shut off the psychosocial aspects of the self when choosing to pursue an advanced degree. Lovitts (2001) noted that a lack of social integration, not academic failure, was the primary cause for attrition. Student affairs professionals have much to offer the graduate and professional student population and should not leave graduate and professional education solely to the purview of academic departments.

Implications for Practice

What does this information mean for educators working with graduate and professional students? We draw your attention back to the practices identified by Pontius and Harper in Chapter Four. Each of the chapters in this volume identifies strategies and practices that fall very much in line with these good practices. How you move forward with the information contained here depends on your institution.

As a first step, think about your location, your campus culture, and its openness to innovation. If your campus is ready to think about a different level of student services for graduate and professional students, Step Two entails finding out who your students are, what they need, and what they think about their current experiences. With Step Three, identify the most salient needs and the appropriate people to address them, and begin to create the human network. Step Four calls for the development of programs designed to meet the identified, and agreed-on, needs and to achieve desired outcomes. These programs are implemented in Step Five. Finally, Step Six marks a return to assessment, checking in to see if the programs are meeting student needs and generating the desired outcomes. If your campus is not ready for a major overhaul, think about where small changes might be initiated, find others concerned with the experience of graduate and professional students, and begin the conversation.

Implications for Research

It has been a challenge to focus on graduate and professional education, in all its variability. A number of areas of graduate education require additional research. First, it is time to revisit the educational and societal outcomes of master's education, particularly since the advent of numerous online master's programs. Lacking additional evidence, we must assume that as Conrad, Haworth, and Millar (1993) indicated, master's education is successful in meeting the needs of students and in serving its societal role. However, the data from this study are over fifteen years old, and much has changed in that time. Second, while Phye and McGuire provided an enlightening glimpse into the complexities of meeting the needs of students in medicine and law, more research is needed in the area of professional school student services and the experiences of professional students.

Third, although we have tried to be inclusive of the heterogeneous population that is graduate and professional students, it constitutes a difficult task. Specific populations such as women, students of color, GLBTQ, and international students might experience more barriers to success in graduate and professional programs. Research is needed that identifies these barriers for students and provides concrete strategies to campuses for assessing their campus climate, breaking down barriers, and providing support to students.

Finally, because of the heterogeneity of the population and the variety of learning environments, it is important to assess the needs and experiences of, and outcomes for, students on your campus. Information on the experiences of students elsewhere can inform and guide your work to meet the needs of your campus graduate and professional population but should not stand in place of institutional data.

Conclusion

In graduate and professional education, calls for reform, innovation, or recognition of the student experience beyond the academic basics can seem to have little impact. In fact, efforts to improve graduate education can feel much like throwing pebbles at Stonehenge. Strong, durable, withstanding, Stonehenge, much like the academy, will not fall; pebbles will not substantially alter its configuration. However, each pebble thrown—each new program, practice, or changed student—wears away layers of stone, gradually giving new form to the stone. This volume, like others before it, is a pebble, a call for change, for innovation, for improved student experiences, for responsibility in the academy. It is a call to all educators, those in academic affairs and student affairs, and to students themselves, to be advocates for improvements in graduate and professional education. It is a call to transform Stonehenge.

References

Atkinson, C. *True Confessions of a Ph.D.* Edinboro, Pa.: Edinboro Educational Press, 1939.

Austin, A. E. "Preparing the Next Generation of Faculty: Graduate School as Socialization to the Academic Career." *Journal of Higher Education*, 2002, 73, 94–122.

Conrad, C., Haworth, J. G., and Millar, S. B. *A Silent Success: Master's Education in the United States.* Baltimore, Md.: Johns Hopkins University Press, 1993.

Katz, J., and Hartnett, R. T. *Scholars in the Making: The Development of Graduate and Professional Students.* Cambridge, Mass.: Ballinger, 1976.

Lovitts, B. E. *Leaving the Ivory Tower: The Causes and Consequences of Departure from Doctoral Study.* Lanham, Md.: Rowman and Littlefield, 2001.

Pelikan, J. *Scholarship and Its Survival: Questions on the Idea of Graduate Education.* Princeton, N.J.: Princeton University Press, 1983.

Rees, C. J. *Graduate Education in the Land-Grant Colleges and Universities.* Baltimore, Md.: Division of Graduate Studies, Association of Land-Grant Colleges and State Universities, 1962.

MELANIE J. GUENTZEL *is director of graduate student services at St. Cloud State University and a doctoral candidate in student affairs administration and research at the University of Iowa.*

BECKI ELKINS NESHEIM *is director of institutional research at Cornell College in Mt. Vernon, Iowa.*

INDEX

Back Issue/Subscription Order Form

Copy or detach and send to:
Jossey-Bass, A Wiley Imprint, 989 Market Street, San Francisco CA, 94103-1741

Call or fax toll-free: Phone 888-378-2537 6:30AM – 3PM PST; Fax 888-481-2665

Back Issues: Please send me the following issues at $28 each
(Important: please include ISBN number for each issue.)

_____

_____

_____

$ _____   Total for single issues

$ _____   SHIPPING CHARGES: SURFACE   Domestic Canadian
                                      First Item $5.00 $6.00
                                      Each Add'l Item $3.00 $1.50
                     For next-day and second-day delivery rates, call the number listed above.

Subscriptions   Please __ start __ renew my subscription to *New Directions for Student Services* for the year 2_____ at the following rate:

U.S.	__ Individual $80	__ Institutional $195
Canada	__ Individual $80	__ Institutional $235
All Others	__ Individual $104	__ Institutional $269

**For more information about online subscriptions visit
www.wileyinterscience.com**

$ Total single issues and subscriptions (Add appropriate sales tax
              for your state for single issue orders. No sales tax for U.S.
——————— subscriptions. Canadian residents, add GST for subscriptions and
              single issues.)

__Payment enclosed (U.S. check or money order only)

__VISA __ MC __ AmEx Card #_____Exp.Date_____

Signature ————————————————— Day Phone _____

__Bill Me (U.S. institutional orders only. Purchase order required.)

Purchase order # ——————————————————————
                 Federal Tax ID13559302   **GST 89102 8052**

Name_____

Address _____

_____

Phone _____ E-mail _____

For more information about Jossey-Bass, visit our Web site at www.josseybass.com

OTHER TITLES AVAILABLE IN THE
New Directions for Student Services Series
JOHN H. SCHUH, EDITOR-IN-CHIEF
ELIZABETH J. WHITT, ASSOCIATE EDITOR

SS114 **Understanding Students in Transition: Trends and Issues**
Frankie Santos Laanan
This volume is designed for practitioners (in student services, teaching, or administration) seeking to understand the changing realities of today's diverse, complex college students. It includes recommendations for research, practice, and policy. The research and practical examples can be applied to multiple student populations: recent high school graduates, community college transfers, and older adults returning to education.
ISBN: 0-7879-8679-8

SS113 **Gambling on Campus**
George S. McClellan, Thomas W. Hardy, Jim Caswell
Gambling has become a serious concern on college campuses, fueled by the surge of online gaming and the national poker craze, and is no longer a fringe activity. This informative issue includes perspectives from students, suggestions for research, frameworks for campus policy development, and case studies of education and intervention. Anyone interested in supporting student success must be informed about gambling on campus.
ISBN: 0-7879-8597-X

SS112 **Technology in Student Affairs: Supporting Student Learning and Services**
Kevin Kruger
Information technology has helped create a 24/7 self-service way for students to interact with campus administrative functions, whether they're on campus or distance learners. And new technologies could move beyond administrative into student learning and development. This volume is not a review of current technology in student affairs. Rather, it focuses on how technology is changing the organization of student affairs, how to use it effectively, and how lines are blurring between campus-based and distance learning.
ISBN: 0-7879-8362-4

SS111 **Gender Identity and Sexual Orientation: Research, Policy, and Personal Perspectives**
Ronni L. Sanlo
Lesbian, gay, bisexual, and transgender people have experienced homophobia, discrimination, exclusion, and marginalization in the academy, from subtle to overt. Yet LGBT people have been a vital part of the history of American higher education. This volume describes current issues, research, and policies, and it offers ways for institutions to support and foster the success of LGBT students, faculty, and staff.
ISBN: 0-7879-8328-4

SS110 **Developing Social Justice Allies**
Robert D. Reason, Ellen M. Broido, Tracy L. Davis, Nancy J. Evans
Social justice allies are individuals from dominant groups (for example, whites, heterosexuals, men) who work to end the oppression of target group members (people of color, homosexuals, women). Student affairs professionals have a history of philosophical commitment to social justice, and this volume strives to provide the theoretical foundation and practical strategies to encourage the development of social justice and civil rights allies among students and colleagues.
ISBN: 0-7879-8077-3

SS109   **Serving Native American Students**
Mary Jo Tippeconnic Fox, Shelly C. Lowe, George S. McClellan
The increasing Native American enrollment on campuses nationwide is
something to celebrate; however, the retention rate for Native American
students is the lowest in higher education, a point of tremendous concern.
This volume's authors—most of them Native American—address topics such
as enrollment trends, campus experiences, cultural traditions, student
services, ignorance about Indian country issues, expectations of tribal
leaders and parents, and other challenges and opportunities encountered by
Native students.
ISBN: 0-7879-7971-6

SS108   **Using Entertainment Media in Student Affairs Teaching and Practice**
Deanna S. Forney, Tony W. Cawthon
Reaching all students may require going beyond traditional methods,
especially in the out-of-classroom environments typical to student affairs.
Using films, music, television shows, and popular books can help students
learn. This volume—good for both practitioners and educators—shares
effective approaches to using entertainment media to facilitate
understanding of general student development, multiculturalism, sexual
orientation, gender issues, leadership, counseling, and more.
ISBN: 0-7879-7926-0

SS107   **Developing Effective Programs and Services for College Men**
Gar E. Kellom
This volume's aim is to better understand the challenges facing college men,
particularly at-risk men. Topics include enrollment, retention, academic
performance, women's college perspectives, men's studies perspectives,
men's health issues, emotional development, and spirituality. Delivers
recommendations and examples about programs and services that improve
college men's learning experiences and race, class, and gender awareness.
ISBN: 0-7879-7772-1

SS106   **Serving the Millennial Generation**
Michael D. Coomes, Robert DeBard
Focuses on the next enrollment boom, students born after 1981, known as
the Millennial generation. Examines these students' attitudes, beliefs, and
behaviors, and makes recommendations to student affairs practitioners for
working with them. Discusses historical and cultural influences that shape
generations, demographics, teaching and learning patterns of Millennials,
and how student affairs can best educate and serve them.
ISBN: 0-7879-7606-7

SS105   **Addressing the Unique Needs of Latino American Students**
Anna M. Ortiz
Explores the experiences of the fast-growing population of Latinos in higher
education, and what these students need from student affairs. This volume
examines the influence of the Latino family, socioeconomic levels, cultural
barriers, and other factors to understand the challenges faced by Latinos.
Discusses administration, student groups, community colleges, support
programs, cultural identity, Hispanic-Serving Institutions, and more.
ISBN: 0-7879-7479-X

SS104   **Meeting the Needs of African American Women**
Mary F. Howard-Hamilton
Identifies and explores the critical needs for African American women as
students, faculty, and administrators. This volume introduces theoretical
frameworks and practical applications for addressing challenges; discusses

identity and spirituality; explores the importance of programming support in recruitment and retention; describes the benefits of mentoring; and provides illuminating case studies of black women's issues in higher education. ISBN: 0-7879-7280-0

SS103   **Contemporary Financial Issues in Student Affairs**
John H. Schuh
This volume addresses the challenging financial situation facing higher education and offers creative solutions for student affairs staff. Topics include the differences between public and private institutions in funding student activities, how to demonstrate financial accountability to stakeholders, plus ways to address budget challenges in student unions, health centers, campus recreation, counseling centers, and student housing. ISBN: 0-7879-7173-1

SS102   **Meeting the Special Needs of Adult Students**
Deborah Kilgore, Penny J. Rice
This volume examines the ways student services professionals can best help adult learners. Chapters highlight the specific challenges that adult enrollment brings to traditional four-year and postgraduate institutions, which are often focused on the traditional-aged student experience. Explaining that adult students are typically involved in campus life in different ways than younger students are, the volume provides student services professionals with good guidance on serving an ever-growing population. ISBN: 0-7879-6991-5

SS101   **Planning and Achieving Successful Student Affairs Facilities Projects**
Jerry Price
Provides student affairs professionals with an examination of critical facilities issues by exploring the experiences of their colleagues. Illustrates that students' educational experiences are affected by residence halls, student unions, dining services, recreation and wellness centers, and campus grounds, and that student affairs professionals make valuable contributions to the success of campus facility projects. Covers planning, budgeting, collaboration, and communication through case studies and lessons learned. ISBN: 0-7879-6847-1

SS100   **Student Affairs and External Relations**
Mary Beth Snyder
Building positive relations with external constituents is as important in student affairs work as it is in any other university or college division. This issue is a long-overdue resource of ideas, strategies, and information aimed at making student affairs leaders more effective in their interactions with important off-campus partners, supporters, and agencies. Chapter authors explore the current challenges facing the student services profession as well as the emerging opportunities worthy of student affairs interest. ISBN: 0-7879-6342-9

SS99   **Addressing Contemporary Campus Safety Issues**
Christine K. Wilkinson, James A. Rund
Provided for practitioners as a resource book for both historical and evolving issues, this guide covers hazing, parental partnerships, and collaborative relationships between universities and the neighboring community. Addressing a new definition of a safe campus environment, the editors have identified topics such as the growth in study abroad, the implications of increased usage of technology on campus, and campus response to September 11. In addition, large-scale crisis responses to student riots and

multiple campus tragedies have been described in case studies. The issue speaks to a more contemporary definition of a safe campus environment that addresses not only physical safety issues but also those of a psychological nature, a more diverse student body, and quality of life.
ISBN: 0-7879-6341-0

SS98   **The Art and Practical Wisdom of Student Affairs Leadership**
Jon Dalton, Marguerite McClinton
This issue collects reflections, stories, and advice about the art and practice of student affairs leadership. Ten senior student affairs leaders were asked to maintain a journal and record their personal reflections on practical wisdom they have gained in the profession. The authors looked inside themselves to provide personal and candid insight into the convictions and values that have guided them in their work and lives.
ISBN: 0-7879-6340-2

SS97   **Working with Asian American College Students**
Marylu K. McEwen, Corinne Maekawa Kodama, Alvin N. Alvarez, Sunny Lee, Christopher T. H. Liang
Highlights the diversity of Asian American college students, analyzes the "model minority" myth and the stereotype of the "perfidious foreigner," and points out the need to consider the racial identity and racial consciousness of Asian American students. Various authors propose a model of Asian American student development, address issues of Asian Americans who are at educational risk, discuss the importance of integration and collaboration between student affairs and Asian American studies programs, and offer strategies for developing socially conscious Asian American student leaders.
ISBN: 0-7879-6292-9S